Opening up
1 Thessalonians

TIM SHENTON

DayOne

The importance of Thessalonica in the history of early Christianity cannot be overestimated since its strategic position meant that the gospel could spread east throughout Asia and west to the city of Rome. Paul and his companions had spent barely three weeks there (Acts 17:2) before they were forced to leave, but the visit, nevertheless, was a great success for the gospel.

However, the Gentile converts had not had time to receive the basic teaching on Christianity which was necessary, and in this letter Paul deals with some of these issues—the equality of God the Father and the Son, the need for holiness of life, and practical questions relating to sexual behaviour and to the doctrine of the second coming of Christ.

Tim Shenton handles these and other matters in a clear and concise manner, and draws out the practical implications for Christian living today. His exposition is readable and informative with relevant quotations and illustrations which make it a useful tool both for the individual Christian and for group study.

Peter Williams,
Southbourne Evangelical Church, Bournemouth, England

© Day One Publications 2006
First printed 2006

Unless otherwise indicated, Scripture quotations in this publication are from the Holy Bible: New International Version (NIV), copyright ©1973, 1978, 1984, International Bible Society. Used by permission of Hodder and Stoughton, a member of the Hodder Headline Group. All rights reserved.

British Library Cataloguing in Publication Data available

Published by Day One Publications
Ryelands Road, Leominster, HR6 8NZ
Telephone 01568 613 740   FAX 01568 611 473

email—sales@dayone.co.uk
web site—www.dayone.co.uk
North American—e-mail-sales@dayonebookstore.com
North American web site—www.dayonebookstore.com

All rights reserved
No part of this publication may be reproduced, or stored in a retrieval system, or transmitted, in any form or by any means, mechanical, electronic, photocopying, recording or otherwise, without the prior permission of Day One Publications.

Designed by Steve Devane and printed by Gutenberg Press, Malta

	Overview	8
	Setting the scene	10
❶	Paul's greeting (1:1-3)	13
❷	Utterly transformed (1:4-10)	18
❸	Paul's defence (2:1-6)	26
❹	The love of Christ (2:7-12)	34
❺	Suffering for the word of God (2:13-16)	42
❻	Paul's love for the Thessalonians (2:17-20)	49
❼	Faith and persecution (3:1-5)	53
❽	Good news (3:6-10)	61
❾	A remarkable petition (3:11-13)	69
❿	Living to please God (4:1-8)	75
⓫	Love and ambition (4:9-12)	81
⓬	The second coming of Christ (4:13-18)	87
⓭	Sons of the light (5:1-11)	94
⓮	Love one another (5:12-15)	102
⓯	The will of God (5:16-22)	108
⓰	God is faithful (5:23-28)	113
	Additional resources	118

List of Bible abbreviations

THE OLD TESTAMENT

		1 Chr.	1 Chronicles	Dan.	Daniel
		2 Chr.	2 Chronicles	Hosea	Hosea
Gen.	Genesis	Ezra	Ezra	Joel	Joel
Exod.	Exodus	Neh.	Nehemiah	Amos	Amos
Lev.	Leviticus	Esth.	Esther	Obad.	Obadiah
Num.	Numbers	Job	Job	Jonah	Jonah
Deut.	Deuteronomy	Ps.	Psalms	Micah	Micah
Josh.	Joshua	Prov.	Proverbs	Nahum	Nahum
Judg.	Judges	Eccles.	Ecclesiastes	Hab.	Habakkuk
Ruth	Ruth	S.of.S.	Song of Solomon	Zeph.	Zephaniah
1 Sam.	1 Samuel	Isa.	Isaiah	Hag.	Haggai
2 Sam.	2 Samuel	Jer.	Jeremiah	Zech.	Zechariah
1 Kings	1 Kings	Lam.	Lamentations	Mal.	Malachi
2 Kings	2 Kings	Ezek.	Ezekiel		

THE NEW TESTAMENT

		Gal.	Galatians	Heb.	Hebrews
		Eph.	Ephesians	James	James
Matt.	Matthew	Phil.	Philippians	1 Peter	1 Peter
Mark	Mark	Col.	Colossians	2 Peter	2 Peter
Luke	Luke	1 Thes.	1 Thessalonians	1 John	1 John
John	John	2 Thes.	2 Thessalonians	2 John	2 John
Acts	Acts	1 Tim.	1 Timothy	3 John	3 John
Rom.	Romans	2 Tim.	2 Timothy	Jude	Jude
1 Cor.	1 Corinthians	Titus	Titus	Rev.	Revelation
2 Cor.	2 Corinthians	Philem.	Philemon		

Overview

Our attention is first directed to the city of Thessalonica in Acts 17 on the second missionary journey of Paul and his friends. It features prominently in the New Testament.

After Paul and Silas had been persecuted for their faith in Philippi, they travelled along one of the most famous Roman military roads, the Egnatian Way, through Amphipolis and Apollonia, a journey of about a hundred miles, before arriving in Thessalonica. Cassander, who named it after his wife, a half-sister of Alexander the Great, founded Thessalonica in 315 BC. When Rome organized Macedonia into a province in 146 BC, Thessalonica was made its capital, and it soon became the second largest city of that area (Philippi being the largest). As a 'free' city (42 BC) it had its own government. It was situated at the head of the Thermaic Gulf, a commercially strategic position, and with its fine harbour it served as a seaport for the rich agricultural plains of Macedonia.

OPENING UP 1 THESSALONIANS

Setting the scene

Most of the Thessalonians were Greeks, although many Orientals and some Romans lived among them. A large Jewish colony had also been attracted by the commerce of the city.

Paul and Silas, along with Timothy, arrived in the city in AD 50. Following his usual custom, Paul went into the synagogue and for three Sabbath days reasoned with the congregation from the Scriptures, 'explaining and proving that the Christ had to suffer and rise from the dead. "This Jesus I am proclaiming to you is the Christ," he said' (Acts 17:3).

Paul did not spend time talking about the city of Thessalonica and its commercial advantages, or enter into a debate with the local politicians; rather he focused attention on the Saviour of the world. His message was always the same: Jesus Christ and him crucified. As a result some of the Jews believed that this Jesus was the promised Messiah and 'joined Paul and Silas, as did a large number of God-fearing Greeks and not a few prominent women' (Acts 17:4). They left the synagogue and assembled in Jason's house, where Paul and Silas lodged.

Whenever God moves in saving power, opposition arises. Some of the Jews became jealous and rounded up various bad characters from the market place, formed a mob and started a riot in the city. They rushed to Jason's house in search of Paul and Silas in order to bring them out to the crowd, but they did not find them there. Instead they dragged Jason and some other brothers before the city officials, accusing them of being the men 'who have caused trouble all over the world... They are all defying Caesar's decrees, saying that there is another king, one called Jesus' (Acts 17:6-7). The crowd and city officials were thrown into turmoil. On the one hand, they had to take notice of such a serious charge; on the other, they had no evidence with which to convict the accused men, so they put Jason and the others on bail and let them go.

> Paul focused attention on the Saviour of the world. His message was always the same: Jesus Christ and him crucified.

Paul and Silas, following Jesus' injunction, 'When you are persecuted in one place, flee to another' (Matt. 10:23), slipped away at night to Berea.

Paul was greatly distressed that he had to leave a newly formed church in Thessalonica and yearned to see them again. When he could stand it no longer, he sent Timothy from Athens back to Thessalonica to comfort them in the midst of their persecutions. Timothy later joined Paul in Corinth and gave him an encouraging report about their progress in the faith. Paul was delighted and wrote his epistle to them from Corinth during his second missionary journey in AD 51.

FOR FURTHER STUDY

1. Read Acts 17:1-10. Were Paul and Silas right to escape from Thessalonica? Should we interpret his actions as cowardice, common sense or obedience to God's word? Can you name other occasions when Paul fled from dangerous situations?
2. Read the last few verses of each chapter of 1 Thessalonians. What is one of the main themes of the epistle?

TO THINK ABOUT AND DISCUSS

1. Why is it so important for Christians to focus on Jesus Christ? What sometimes distracts us from preaching 'Jesus Christ and him crucified'?
2. In Thessalonica there were Greeks, Romans, Orientals and Jews. Is the Christian message always the same, or should we try to adapt it to different nationalities? Read 1 Corinthians 9:20-22. What did Paul mean when he said, 'I have become all things to all men so that by all possible means I might save some'?
3. Paul loved the Thessalonians. How did he express his love for them? How do you express your love for other Christians?

1 Paul's greeting

(1:1-3)

It is clear throughout the letter that Paul loved the believers at Thessalonica in both a maternal and paternal way. They were his spiritual children and he was determined to look after them in every way he could.

Standing together (v. 1)

Paul's opening greeting is brief and he makes no mention of his apostleship, because no one in Thessalonica doubted his authority. The believers knew he was a man appointed and sent by God to proclaim the gospel.

Paul introduces Silas and Timothy as his fellow workers in the gospel. All three men were equally concerned about the spiritual welfare of the church and Paul wanted to stress that they were standing together in unity and fighting for a common cause. Paul was never a man to push himself forward in front of others. He was a humble man who wanted the Thessalonians to appreciate his co-workers.

Paul was writing to the 'church' of the Thessalonians, fully recognizing them as a body of believers, made up of Jews and Gentiles, who had been called out of darkness into God's wonderful light. These believers were 'in God the Father and the Lord Jesus Christ'. They were firmly rooted in both the first and second persons of the Holy Trinity.

Every Christian has fellowship with God the Father through God the Son. It is not possible for a believer to have the Father without the Son, or the Son without the Father. The apostle John wrote, 'No one who denies the Son has the Father; whoever acknowledges the Son has the Father also' (1 John 2:23). The two persons are inseparable and indivisibly one.

Some early manuscripts have 'grace and peace to you' from God the Father and the Lord Jesus Christ. Grace is the unmerited favour of God in rescuing sinners from the wrath to come, transforming them by the power of the Spirit into the image of Christ and securing their entrance into heaven. The fruit of grace is peace. Every Christian has been reconciled to God and is now at peace with him. The enmity that existed between the two parties has been replaced with the embrace of love. Enemies have become friends. All the blessings of grace and peace come from God the Father through the Lord Jesus Christ.

Praying together (v. 2)

Paul was a man who practised what he preached. To the Philippians he said, 'Do not be anxious about anything, but in everything, by prayer and petition, with thanksgiving, present your requests to God' (Phil. 4:6). Here he is praying daily and earnestly, with Silas and Timothy, for his friends in Thessalonica and thanking God for the work of salvation that had been brought about in their lives.

Matthew Henry, the great Bible commentator, was once attacked by thieves and robbed of his purse. That evening he wrote in his diary, 'Let me be thankful first, because I was never robbed before; second, because, although they took my purse, they did not take my life; third, because, although they took everything, it was not much; and fourth, because it was I who was robbed, and not I who robbed.'

Our great duty as Christians is to overflow with gratitude for the daily grace and love that God lavishes on us. Where, for instance, would we be today if God had not rescued us from the broad road that leads to destruction? The more we understand what our redemption means, the more we shall lift up our voices in heartfelt praise to our Saviour.

Living the Christian life together (v. 3)

After a general comment about prayer to encourage the Thessalonians, Paul specifically mentions the three great foundation stones of the Christian life that he had been remembering 'before our God and Father': faith, love and hope.

'YOUR WORK PRODUCED BY FAITH.' Faith without works is dead and leads nowhere. There was once a Scotsman who rowed people across a river. On one oar he had carved the word 'faith' and on the other oar he had carved the word 'works'. One day as he was rowing, one of the passengers noticed the carvings and asked him about them. The Scotsman did not reply but pulled in the oar marked 'works' and started to row with only

> Our hope of the final victory, that is assured at Christ's second coming, enables us to persevere through the good times and the bad.

one oar. The boat went round in circles. He then pulled in the oar marked 'faith' and started to row only with the 'works' oar. The boat again went round in circles, but this time in the opposite direction. He then rowed with both oars and reached the other bank safely. Before his passenger got off the boat he said, 'A Christian must row his life using both oars, faith and works. Only then will he reach heaven's shore.' True faith influences the heart and life so that we obey God and serve others. The Thessalonians were acting out their faith in works of compassion and mercy. Here Paul is probably referring to their fearless preaching of the gospel in the midst of persecution.

'YOUR LABOUR PROMPTED BY LOVE.' Faith works by love. In Galatians Paul said, 'The only thing that counts is faith expressing itself through love' (Gal. 5:6). A Christian's heart must be filled with a self-denying and sacrificial love for God and others (agape). The Thessalonians were demonstrating their love for God and for their neighbours by practical acts of service. The apostle John said, 'Dear children, let us not love with words or tongue but with actions and in truth' (1 John 3:18).

'YOUR ENDURANCE INSPIRED BY HOPE IN OUR LORD JESUS CHRIST.' Hope has been compared first to a soldier's helmet, because it protects the mind, and then to the sailor's anchor, because it steadies the heart on the stormy seas of life. Our hope of the final victory, that is assured at Christ's second coming, enables us to persevere through the good times and the bad. The Thessalonians had a well-grounded hope of eternal life and the glory that accompanies it; therefore they could be patient in bearing hardships.

FOR FURTHER STUDY

1. Many great Christians have regarded humility as the number one virtue that we should all possess. Paul was a humble man. Read Philippians 2:5-11 and then name the characteristics of Jesus' humility.
2. There is nothing more vital to the health of a Christian than prayer. It is his lifeblood. Without it he will shrivel up and come to nothing. The famous Welsh preacher, Christmas Evans, said, 'The head, the arms, the limbs, and the whole body of religious duties may be visible, but if secret prayer is not regarded the vital spark is gone, and there remains a breathless corpse.' Study Paul's prayer for the Ephesians in chapter 3:14-21. What did Paul want God to do in the lives of the Ephesians?

TO THINK ABOUT AND DISCUSS

1. Think about your own prayer life in the light of Ephesians 3:14-21. How can it be improved? What opportunities do you have to pray with others?
2. What is faith? What is love? What is hope? Why does Paul say in 1 Corinthians 13:13: 'And now these three remain: faith, hope and love. But the greatest of these is love'? What does he mean?
3. Name three examples of Christ's love as revealed in the gospels.
4. Discuss as a group how you can show more of Christ's love to your neighbours.

2 Utterly transformed

(1:4-10)

The wonderful message of salvation is not simply that we receive eternal life, glorious though that is, but that our lives are utterly transformed by the power of God so that we can live to his glory.

Chosen by God (vv. 4-5)

Paul knew that the Thessalonian Christians had been loved by God from eternity and chosen by him before the creation of the world. In fact, he was so certain of their election that he calls them 'brothers'. But how did he know that God had predestined them for salvation? Because of the success of his ministry among them. The good news of the gospel came to the Thessalonians 'not simply with words', but:

'WITH POWER.' Paul's message was not just an ordinary spoken message; it was a powerful divine message. The words he spoke had that vital and heavenly force behind them that brings salvation. They were words of dynamite that were both destructive and constructive in the sense that they destroyed the idols that had hold of the Thessalonians and, at the same time, turned them around to serve the living and true God (v. 9). Only omnipotence can rescue us from Satan's stronghold. We must never imagine that we wriggled free from the devil's grasp by our own strength or ingenuity, for he had taken us captive to do his will; rather, it was an almighty hand that wrested us from his clutches.

'WITH THE HOLY SPIRIT.' When Paul, Silas and Timothy were preaching, the Holy Spirit anointed them to such a degree that it was as if God was speaking. It is only God the Holy Spirit who enlightens the mind with truth, strikes the conscience with a genuine conviction of sin, softens the heart and makes the gospel effective in the lives of hardened sinners. This is why preachers must preach with the unction of the Holy Spirit; otherwise they will preach 'simply with words'. Paul said to the Corinthians, 'My message and my preaching were not with wise and persuasive words, but with a demonstration of the Spirit's power, so that your faith might not rest on men's wisdom, but on God's power' (1 Cor. 2:4-5). What the church needs today is not fine-sounding sermons that tickle our intellect, delivered by men without the Spirit of God on their ministry, but preachers of power who break rocks into pieces with the hammer of God's word.

'WITH DEEP CONVICTION.' All three men were convinced that God was speaking through them. They were certain that God's word would not return empty, but would accomplish what he desired and achieve the purpose for which it was sent. And they were not disappointed. One of the proofs that a man has been called to the ministry is that there is fruit from his labours. According to Charles Haddon Spurgeon, the prince of preachers, a minister 'must see a measure of conversion work going on under his efforts. How are they sent of God who bring no men to God? Surely it were better to be a mud-raker, or a chimney sweep, than to stand in the ministry as an utterly barren tree. The meanest occupation confers some benefit upon mankind, but the wretched man who occupies the pulpit and never glorifies his God by conversions is a blank, a blot, an eyesore, a mischief. He is not worth the salt he eats, much less his bread.' Strong words, but how can we disagree with them?

There is no point in preaching the truth if we are living a lie. The three evangelists backed up their message with lives of love and purity. 'You know how we lived among you for your sake.' This personal reference is partly to counter the attacks of the unbelieving Jews, who were questioning the integrity of the preachers and at the same time undermining the Thessalonians' faith and assurance of salvation. The question we must ask ourselves is: Do we preach the gospel with our words and with our lives? Every Christian must remember the well-known saying: 'Actions speak louder than words.'

A model to follow (vv. 6-10)

In response to Paul and his friends' preaching and example, the Thessalonians became 'imitators of us and of the Lord', which was a visible evidence of their election. In imitating Paul, a disciple of Christ, they were imitating the Lord. The outcome of this was that they became a model for others to follow. In other words, the imitators became the imitated! One thing is clear—our actions and attitudes are watched and followed.

Welcoming the message

Joy and persecution often go together in the Bible. Jesus said, 'Blessed are you when people insult you, and persecute you and falsely say all kinds of evil against you because of me. Rejoice and be glad, because great is your reward in heaven' (Matt. 5:11-12). Peter says something similar: 'Rejoice that you participate in the sufferings of Christ, so that you may be overjoyed when his glory is revealed' (1 Peter 4:13).

Only true faith and 'the joy given by the Holy Spirit' can welcome the gospel message 'in spite of severe suffering'. Those whose faith is a sham will not persevere through the fires of affliction. They are like seed sown on rocky places; they 'hear the word and at once receive it with joy. But since they have no root, they last only a short time. When trouble or persecution comes because of the word, they quickly fall away' (Mark 4:16-17).

Spreading the message

The example of the Thessalonians echoed throughout

Macedonia and Achaia and beyond, and encouraged 'all the believers' to stand firm through the storms of persecution and not to give up. What a testimony: 'your faith in God has become known everywhere'! Without them really knowing it, they had become missionaries and evangelists to the world by report.

Christians should never panic if they are required to suffer for their faith. Many of the early Christians viewed suffering as a gift from God. They expected persecution and regarded it as a badge of honour. John Wesley was riding along a road one day when he was horrified at the thought that he had not been persecuted for three whole days. Not a brick or an egg had been thrown at him during that time. Alarmed, he stopped his horse and exclaimed, 'Can it be that I have sinned, and am backslidden?' He slipped from his horse and fell on his knees, crying out to God to show him where, if any, there had been a fault.

A rough fellow, on the other side of the hedge, heard Wesley's prayer and, recognizing the preacher, said to himself, 'I'll fix that Methodist preacher.' He picked up a rock and threw it at him. It missed its mark and fell harmlessly beside Wesley, who leaped to his feet joyfully exclaiming, 'Thank God, it's all right. I still have his presence.'

It is through suffering that God strengthens our faith and proves it to be genuine. A tree when it is blown from side to side by strong winds digs its roots more firmly into the ground. So a Christian, when he is tossed to and fro by the winds of persecution, becomes more firmly rooted in Christ.

Living the message

True repentance is a deliberate turning from sin to God. The Thessalonians had deliberately 'turned to God from idols to serve the living and true God'. They had shunned their idols and the deities they represented and received the supreme Creator God as their Saviour. They had turned their backs on the unreal dreams of men to accept the true God. Superstition and fear had been thrown away and replaced by a determination to serve the God they had so long rejected. How true is the saying: 'Man repents, God renews'!

In Psalm 115 there is a poignant description of the impotency of idols in contrast to the God of heaven, who 'does whatever pleases him'.

> But their idols are silver and gold,
> made by the hands of men.
> They have mouths, but cannot speak,
> eyes, but they cannot see;
> they have ears, but cannot hear,
> noses, but they cannot smell;
> they have hands, but cannot feel,
> feet, but they cannot walk;
> nor can they utter a sound with their throats.
> Those who make them will be like them,
> and so will all who trust in them
> (Ps. 115:4-8).

Waiting for the Saviour

The word 'wait' means a sustained expectation. Even though the time of Christ's return is unknown, the Thessalonians were ready for his appearance from heaven. They had been transformed because of his first coming, now they were looking forward with patience and confidence to his second coming.

They knew he would come again because God had 'raised him from the dead'. They did not worship a dead Messiah, but one who is alive and waiting for his Father's command to return. This Jesus is the Saviour 'who rescues us from the coming wrath'. Wrath is God's eternal and settled indignation against sin.

There is a day that is fast approaching when all the nations will be gathered before the Son of Man, 'and he will separate the people one from another as a shepherd separates the sheep from the goats'. To the sheep he will say, 'Come, you who are blessed by my Father; take your inheritance, the kingdom prepared for you since the creation of the world.' To the goats he will say, 'Depart from me, you who are cursed, into the eternal fire prepared for the devil and his angels' (Matt. 25:31-46).

We must never forget that the day of wrath will soon be upon us. This is not a popular message in our modern world where the love of God is often over-emphasized to the exclusion of everything else; but as surely as you are reading these words, so that day will come, when 'everything will be destroyed'.

In view of its coming, what kind of people ought we to be? We 'ought to live holy and godly lives' as we look forward to the day of God and speed its coming (2 Peter 3:11-12).

FOR FURTHER STUDY

1. All Christians are 'loved by God'. Read Romans 8:31-39 and try to understand more fully what it means to be loved by God. What does it means to be 'more than conquerors through him who loved us'? Paul was convinced that nothing in all creation 'will be able to separate us from the love of God that is in Christ Jesus our Lord'. Is he right, and if so, why?
2. What does it means to preach 'with a demonstration of the Spirit's power' (1 Cor. 2:4-5)?
3. Read Zephaniah 1:14-18. What sort of day will the 'great day of the LORD' be? What are some of the theological difficulties that Christians might encounter in the way in which they understand the great day of the Lord?

TO THINK ABOUT AND DISCUSS

1. What changes have occurred in your life since you have become a Christian?
2. Do your neighbours know you are a Christian? How does your life differ from the lives of your non-Christian friends?
3. Discuss how Christians should respond to times of suffering and persecution.

3 Paul's defence

(2:1-6)

Paul was ready to defend himself and his friends, Silas and Timothy, against the attacks of the Jews, who were endeavouring to portray them as deluded individuals intent on tricking others. If the reputation of the messengers can be damaged, then their message is less likely to be trusted.

Paul's courage (vv. 1-2)

The Thessalonians knew very well that Paul's visit to them was 'not a failure'. Indeed, they had firsthand knowledge of its success and how the gospel had transformed their lives. The word translated 'failure' means 'empty' or 'hollow'. When the missionaries had visited the Thessalonians, their hands were not empty and their message was not void of power or reality. They came not to take away honesty and truth from them, but to give them the message of the God of truth.

Paul and Silas had 'suffered' terribly in Philippi. After Paul had exorcized from a slave girl 'a spirit by which she predicted the future', both men were dragged into the market place to face the authorities. They were falsely accused of advocating unlawful customs, 'severely flogged' and thrown into prison, where they were put in the inner cell and their feet fastened in the stocks (Acts 16).

In spite of what the two men had suffered at Philippi, they were not afraid of entering Thessalonica and preaching the same gospel. The insults and injuries they had received in no way daunted them or tempted them to compromise the message God had given them.

What we need today is that courageous outspokenness that comes from a confidence in God and the gospel, a holy boldness that is not shaken even when others oppose us. The great preacher, Rowland Hill, was quite right when he said, 'Cold, formal, halfway sermons neither give half the offence, nor do half the good as those which are plain and faithful. Truth can best defend itself without the assistance of our low cunning, in attempting to make it palatable to the carnal mind.

> What we need today is that courageous outspokenness that comes from a confidence in God and the gospel, a holy boldness that is not shaken even when others oppose us.

'Rash preaching always disgusts; timid preaching does nothing but leave poor souls fast asleep; while bold preaching, if delivered under an affectionate love to the souls of men, and with a humble desire to promote the glory of God, is the only preaching that is owned and blessed of Him.'

David Simpson of Macclesfield once preached a sermon entitled *Marriage Honourable, Whoredom Damnable*, in which he stated in no uncertain terms that 'all who indulge to the gratification of their carnal inclinations, in any other way than that of legal matrimony, are guilty of uncleanness, adultery, or fornication. And we are assured in the most solemn, serious, and positive manner, in different parts of the word of God, that none such have any share, or inheritance, in the kingdom of Christ and of God.

'Next time then, O sinner, next time you are guilty of any criminal indulgence; next time, and every time you commit the unclean act; next time you pollute your body, or defile your lips with foolish, impure, unchristian, unmanly conversation, remember, O remember, that the drawn sword of divine justice is suspended over your guilty head. Remember, that you are selling your all, your eternal all—for what? The gratification of a vile lust. Remember that you are plunging yourself in endless misery and ruin—for what? Alas, for what! 'Tis a shame even to mention what!

'Repent like David—weep like Peter—love like Magdalene—live like the Redeemer of the world. But if instead of this you harden your neck, persist in your unclean courses, and live in contempt both of divine and human laws, your case is desperate. You will live pitied and despised by the virtuous and the good. You will die in disgrace. You will rise in shame. You will be struck with tenfold confusion before the bar of God.'

In the twenty-first century we need men of holy boldness like Simpson to preach the old-fashioned gospel without compromise or fear.

Paul, Silas and Timothy remained faithful 'in spite of strong opposition'. They were God's servants, with God's message, who preached the gospel with God's help. The picture here is of three men exerting themselves to the utmost in a similar way to an athlete who is straining to win an Olympic gold medal. They were prepared to endure all manner of hardships in order to win the Thessalonians to Christ.

Their wholehearted commitment reminds me of Shadrach, Meshach and Abednego. When these three men were about to be thrown into the fiery furnace, they said to Nebuchadnezzar, 'If we are thrown into the blazing furnace, the God we serve is able to save us from it, and he will rescue us from your hand, O king. But even if he does not, we want you to know, O king, that we will not serve your gods or worship the image of gold you have set up' (Dan. 3:17-18).

Wherever the gospel is truly preached, opposition will arise. Therefore let us be strong and put on the whole armour of God, so that we can take our stand against the devil's schemes.

Paul's appeal (vv. 3-6)

Paul's defence reflects the charges that had been made against the three missionaries. He tackles each accusation head on and, being conscious of the sincerity of their actions and words and with full confidence in the gospel, supports the 'appeal' they made. This entreaty did not spring from:

'ERROR.' The apostles were not deceived or mistaken in what they said, but declared the gospel that had come from the highest source of truth—God himself.

'IMPURE MOTIVES.' The message they preached was worthy of its holy author. They were not pretending one thing while intending another.

TRICKERY. In that day there were many so called 'philosophers' who used various tricks to impress their audiences. Not so with Paul. He did not use guile or deceit to capture the people. The message he proclaimed was not a cunningly devised fable that he used for his own profit.

Nor in their efforts to win the Thessalonians did they:

'USE FLATTERY' They did not try to tickle their ears with some cajoling address or excuse their sin; rather, they preached Christ and him crucified.

'PUT ON A MASK TO COVER UP GREED.' They did not use their ministry as a cloak to enrich themselves. They were not like the false prophets who exploited people with stories they had made up in order to satisfy their greed. On the contrary, the missionaries had waived their right to be supported financially. Sadly, in our own day, there are some who peddle the word of God out of selfish ambition.

LOOK 'FOR PRAISE FROM MEN.' They did not want or need man's approval because they had God's, and that was enough. Their interest was not their own self-importance but the honour of God. In this they were following their Saviour, who had rebuked the persecuting Jews with the words: 'I do not accept praise from men, but I know you. I know that you do not have the love of God in your hearts. I have come in my Father's name, and you do not accept me; but if someone else comes in his own name, you will accept him. How can you believe if you accept praise from another, yet make no effort to obtain the praise that comes from the only God?' (John 5:41-44).

Paul and his associates were men 'approved by God' and 'entrusted with the gospel'. They had been tried and tested and found worthy to preach the good news. They had received divine approbation, not because of some innate worthiness, but because of God's grace. In 2 Corinthians Paul makes a similar defence: 'We have renounced secret and shameful ways; we do not use deception, nor do we distort the word of God. On the contrary, by setting forth the truth plainly we commend ourselves to every man's conscience in the sight of God' (2 Cor. 4:2).

> The missionaries had waived their right to be supported financially. Sadly, in our own day, there are some who peddle the word of God out of selfish ambition.

In all that they said and did, they knew that the omniscient God 'tests our hearts'. Man looks at the outward appearance but the Lord looks at the heart. No impure motive or crafty expedient escapes his all-seeing gaze. He is the invisible witness of all things. He knows all our thoughts, motives and desires. He searches our inmost being.

'O LORD, you have searched me
and you know me.
You know when I sit and when I rise;

you perceive my thoughts from afar.
You discern my going out and my lying down;
you are familiar with all my ways.
Before a word is on my tongue
you know it completely, O LORD'
(Ps. 139:1-4).

In view of the omniscience of God, dishonesty for the apostles was unthinkable.

Every minister of the gospel must be above reproach. There must be no hidden skeletons in the cupboard and nothing the enemies of Christ can latch onto to bring the name of Christ into disrepute. They must be, publicly and privately, 'squeaky-clean'.

FOR FURTHER STUDY

1. Why was it necessary for Paul to defend his ministry? Couldn't he have ignored the false accusations and carried on regardless? Read Galatians 1:11-24. What did Paul say to convince the Galatians that he was an apostle 'sent not from men nor by man, but by Jesus Christ and God the Father'?

2. It is vital that ministers of the gospel are above reproach. What are some of the temptations that might trouble them? Read Matthew 4:1-11. What were the temptations of Jesus and how did he overcome them?

TO THINK ABOUT AND DISCUSS

1. Discuss various ways that you can support the minister of your church.

2. How should the omniscience of God influence our daily lives?

3. Once, when Rowland Hill was descending the pulpit stairs after preaching, a woman rushed up to him and started to praise his sermon. Rowland Hill interrupted her and said, 'That's just what the devil told me as soon as I had finished!' What do you think Rowland Hill meant? Why are we so susceptible to the praises of others and how should we respond when we are praised?

4 The love of Christ

(2:7-12)

Paul is keen to stress how he and his fellow missionaries had treated the Thessalonians, which is partly a defence against those Jews who were criticizing their actions. It is also a challenging example to all who would seek to win others to Christ.

A mother's love (vv. 7-9)

As missionaries sent out by the church with a divine commission, Paul, Silas and Timothy could have insisted upon the importance of their office and exercised their God-given authority with vigour; but they did not want to 'burden' the Thessalonians with their 'rights' and so chose to act differently.

Gentleness

The apostles were 'gentle' among the Thessalonians, 'like a

mother caring for her little children'. Instead of being greedy and demanding respect, they were mild, unselfish and kind in their dealings. When a mother is nursing her child, whom she loves with all her heart, she does not claim the honour that is due her, but is prepared to do anything she can for her precious son or daughter. She warms and cherishes her child. She speaks softly to it. She spends time with it. She lovingly embraces it. She is tender and approachable, and bends over backwards to meet its every need.

Robert Moffat, who became a famous missionary, was leaving home for the first time and his mother walked with him for part of the way. When she could walk no further, she stopped and asked, 'Robert, promise me something.'

'What?' replied the boy.

'Promise me something,' she said again.

'You will have to tell me what it is before I will promise.'

'It is something you can easily do,' she said. 'Promise your mother.'

Robert looked into her face and said, 'Very well, mother, I will do anything you wish.'

She clasped her hands behind his head and gently pulled his face down to hers, saying, 'Robert, you are going out into a wicked world. Begin every day with God. Close every day with God.' Then she kissed him.

Robert Moffat later said that it was his mother's tender kiss that made him a missionary.

The best way to win others to Christ is not to wave the rod of authority over their heads, but to be gentle and kind. When writing to Timothy, Paul said, 'The Lord's servant must not quarrel; instead, he must be kind to everyone …

Those who oppose him he must gently instruct, in the hope that God will grant them repentance leading them to a knowledge of the truth' (2 Tim. 2:24-25). If a mother is stern and aggressive, the child will run from her, but if she is affectionate and kind, it will love her embrace.

Love

Paul and his companions expressed a deep love for the Thessalonians, which moved them to share with their new friends not only the 'gospel of God', but their lives as well. There was a deep and lasting bond between them that was strengthened when the Thessalonians were converted. In all that they did, the missionaries backed up their preaching with a total commitment to those they desired to win to Christ. Their message was not simply empty words, but it was supported by a practical demonstration of God's love.

> In all that they did, the missionaries backed up their preaching with a total commitment to those they desired to win to Christ. Their message was not simply empty words, but it was supported by a practical demonstration of God's love.

If we are to preach the gospel effectively, then we must live out the gospel. Our talents, time and energies must be used to spread the love of Christ. We must not be like the hypocrites, who say one thing and do another. The Pharisees were great talkers and experts at tying up heavy loads to put on men's shoulders, but they themselves would not lift a finger to move them (Matt. 23:4). May what we practise have the result of strengthening the message we preach.

Toil

The Thessalonians knew how hard Paul, Silas and Timothy had worked 'in order not to be a burden to anyone' while they preached the gospel to them. They sacrificed their lives without charge; they toiled to the point of weariness; they struggled against many hardships; they worked long hours, part of the day and part of the night making tents—all in an effort firstly to prove to the Thessalonians that they were not trying to get anything from them, and secondly to maintain their independence while discharging their commission. No one could therefore lay them open to the charge of profiteering, or of using the Thessalonians for their own selfish ends. The three missionaries laid aside every possible hindrance to the gospel.

A father's love (vv. 10-12)

The Thessalonian Christians observed the three missionaries at close quarters and found nothing to criticize in their behaviour. Their testimony was confirmed by the way they lived. Furthermore, God was their witness and he examines the motives and principles of our hearts, and there is nothing hidden from his sight. Even if Paul and his companions had managed to fool the Thessalonians, they could not fool God. They were:

'**HOLY.**' They behaved as men who had been separated to God and his service.

'RIGHTEOUS.' They always strove to do what was right according to the law of God.

'BLAMELESS.' Their conduct was irreproachable before men. They lived without giving cause for scandal or offence.

Surely we should all exert ourselves to the utmost to be like Job: 'This man was blameless and upright; he feared God and shunned evil' (Job 1:1). Everything that in any way casts a shadow on our Christian testimony should be immediately and unreservedly trampled under foot.

Paul loved the Thessalonians as a mother and admonished them as a father, not just publicly in groups, but from house to house. He was concerned for them as individuals and so dealt with them faithfully as a pastor. His fidelity and the manly strength of his counsels were essential for their spiritual progress. They were part of his family, immature in the faith and yet cared for as his 'own children'.

HE ENCOURAGED THEM. He exhorted them to live in a manner pleasing to God, knowing full well there were many obstacles and difficulties along the path to glory that would attempt to trip them up. In Hebrews 3:13, the writer urges us to 'encourage one another daily, as long as it is called Today, so that none of you may be hardened by sin's deceitfulness'. One of the sharpest and hottest darts of the evil one is discouragement, for it causes our hands to go limp and our knees to wobble. According to a legend, the devil once advertised his tools at a public auction. When the buyers assembled, they noticed an oddly shaped tool that was labelled 'Not for sale'. Asked to explain why that was, the devil replied, 'I can spare my other tools, but I cannot spare this one. It is the most useful and effective tool I have. It is called Discouragement, and with it I can work my way into hearts that are otherwise inaccessible. When I get into a man's heart using this tool, the way is open for me to plant anything there I want.' When we are discouraged, it is harder to resist temptation and we can feel like giving up. After the exiles had returned to Jerusalem and were rebuilding the temple, the people living around them set out to discourage them and make them afraid to go on building (Ezra 4:4). Israel's enemies knew the disarming power of discouragement.

> Paul had been comforted in his own troubles by the God of all comfort so that he could comfort those in any trouble with the comfort he had received from God. All the blessings we receive from God are to be used in a way that will relieve and strengthen fellow pilgrims on their journey to heaven.

HE COMFORTED THEM. He did all he could to cheer and support their spirits under hardships and distresses. Paul had been comforted in his own troubles by the God of all comfort so that he could comfort those in any trouble with the comfort he had received from God. All the blessings we receive from God are to be used in a way that will relieve and strengthen fellow pilgrims on their journey to heaven.

HE URGED THEM. A father watching his son run a marathon stands on the side and urges him on, entreating him to make every effort to go as fast as possible and to reach the finish line. So Paul is standing with the Thessalonians and imploring them to throw off the sin that so easily entangles and to run with perseverance the Christian race. He is not going to give up on them.

In all his exhortations Paul wants them to 'live lives worthy of God'. He desires them to walk in harmony with God and in a manner that pleases him who has called them into his 'kingdom and glory'. Although God exercises his kingly rule over his people in the present, this verse is looking to the future when his kingship is fully realized and his glory fully reflected in his people.

In effect Paul is saying to the Thessalonians, 'This is God's message, brought by God's messengers, so that you can live for God's glory on your way to God's kingdom.'

As Christians we must never forget that we are on a journey to God's kingdom of eternal glory. This world is not our home for we are just passing through. May we therefore live as 'aliens and strangers' in reverent fear.

FOR FURTHER STUDY

1. Read 1 Corinthians 13 and give examples of the characteristics of love in the life of Jesus. Why is love greater than faith and hope?
2. There have always been hypocrites in the church and Jesus had some very strong words to say about them. Read Matthew 23. How would you explain to an unbeliever the difference between a hypocrite and a true Christian? Jesus called the teachers of the law and the Pharisees 'blind fools', 'snakes' and 'sons of hell'. Is it permissible for Christians to use such terms when denouncing hypocrites? Explain your answer.

TO THINK ABOUT AND DISCUSS

1. How does a mother's love differ from a father's love?
2. In the last six months, how have you shown Christian love to the members of your family?
3. In 1 John 3:16 the apostle says, 'This is how we know what love is: Jesus Christ laid down his life for us. And we ought to lay down our lives for our brothers.' What does it mean to 'lay down our lives for our brothers' in practical terms? How would our daily lives be changed if every Christian put this verse into practice?
4. Discuss what it means to be 'aliens and strangers in the world' (1 Peter 2:11).

5 Suffering for the word of God

(2:13-16)

Paul and his colleagues turn their attention away from the Thessalonians to the God of the Thessalonians and lift up their hearts in thanksgiving for what he has done.

The word of God (v. 13)

Paul wrote to the Corinthians, 'Always give yourselves fully to the work of the Lord, because you know that your labour in the Lord is not in vain' (1 Cor. 15:58). The three missionaries had given themselves 'fully to the work of the Lord' in Thessalonica and had reaped a harvest of souls. In response they 'thank God continually' for the manner in which the Thessalonians had received the word and the effect it had had on their lives.

The Thessalonians did not accept the gospel 'as the word of men', which is powerless and empty, 'but as … the word of God'. They opened the ears of their hearts and willingly heard and submitted to the preached word, acknowledging it as the voice of God. God clothed his word with authority and the Thessalonians inwardly welcomed it, and proved their acceptance of it by the spiritual fruit it bore in their lives.

When we read or hear God's word we must receive it for what it is, God's word. We must remember that it is holy, wise and just, because its author is holy, wise and just. We should not sit in judgement on it, but allow it to judge the thoughts and attitudes of our hearts and to change our lives. David the Psalmist gives a powerful description of God's word and its effectiveness:

> The law of the Lord is perfect, reviving the soul.
> The statues of the Lord are trustworthy, making wise the simple.
> The precepts of the Lord are right, giving joy to the heart.
> The commands of the Lord are radiant, giving light to the eyes.
> The fear of the Lord is pure, enduring for ever.
> The ordinances of the Lord are sure and altogether righteous.
> They are more precious than gold, than much pure gold;
> they are sweeter than honey, than honey from the comb.
> By them is your servant warned;
> in keeping them there is great reward
> (Ps. 19:7-11).

The word that the Thessalonians had received was 'at work in you who believe', which means it was effective and profitable. The divine origin of the word causes it to work powerfully in all who believe its message. The word 'believe' is in the present tense because it shows the condition we must fulfil if we are to experience the word working in our lives on a daily basis.

Suffering for Christ (vv. 14-16)

The effectiveness of the word of God that had penetrated the hearts of the Thessalonians was proved by their steadfast endurance of persecution. True salvation produces a willingness to suffer for Christ. And this suffering, which so many saints in every generation the world over experience, is a visible sign of the invisible battle that is raging between the devil and the church.

The persecuted

The Thessalonians became 'imitators of God's churches in Judea' who were similarly afflicted. In other words, the suffering of the Thessalonians, which occurred after the missionaries had left and was instigated by the Jews and supported by the Gentiles, meant that the Jewish Christians of Judea and the Gentile believers in Thessalonica were both suffering at the hands of their fellow countrymen.

Paul had firsthand knowledge of the suffering of the 'churches in Judea' because he at one time had been one of their persecutors. This persecution, which brought out a unity of suffering between Jewish and Gentile Christians, was all because they were 'in Christ Jesus', as opposed to other Judean communities. Jesus Christ is the central figure against which violence and hatred are directed.

Paul told Timothy that 'everyone who wants to live a godly life in Christ Jesus will be persecuted' (2 Tim. 3:12). Jesus warned his disciples, 'If they persecuted me, they will persecute you also... They will treat you this way because of my name, for they do not know the One who sent me' (John

15:20, 21). Just as the Lord Jesus was shamefully treated, so his disciples will be treated with contempt. There is no escaping persecution if we are serious about our faith and fully committed to our Saviour. When someone becomes a Christian he turns around and starts walking in the opposite direction to the world. It therefore sets him on a collision course.

The persecutors

Paul gives a damning description of the Jews who, before, during and after the time of Jesus, were intent on opposing God.

THEY 'KILLED THE LORD JESUS AND THE PROPHETS'. This persecution was nothing new for it had gone on during the times of the Old Testament prophets who were mercilessly murdered by the people they were trying to help. Jesus fared no better, for Peter accuses the Jews of killing the 'author of life' (Acts 3:15). If the spotless Lamb of God, who is 'holy, blameless, pure, set apart from sinners, exalted above the heavens' (Heb. 7:26), was murdered, what likelihood have his disciples of escaping persecution?

THEY DROVE OUT THE APOSTLES. They did everything they could to stop the apostles from preaching the word in Thessalonica and elsewhere, literally hounding them wherever they went.

'THEY DISPLEASE GOD.' Murder and persecution are hateful to God. The Jews were doing the exact opposite of what they should have been doing. Instead of glorifying God by turning to his Son in repentance and faith, instead of loving their neighbour as themselves, they used all their energies and efforts to hinder the gospel and pour scorn on the crucified Saviour and his followers.

THEY WERE 'HOSTILE TO ALL MEN'. Moved by the power of bigotry, they violently and persistently opposed anyone who dared to stand up for the name of Christ. All that they did was contrary to nature, humanity and the law of God. They were aggressive and hostile towards 'all men', whether they were Jews or Gentiles.

Why did these men behave in such a way? There was nothing more odious to the Jews than to imagine any kind of salvation for 'Gentile dogs'. The Jews in Jerusalem, for instance, listened quietly to Paul until he said, 'Then the Lord said to me, "Go; I will send you far away to the Gentiles."' Then they 'raised their voices and shouted, "Rid the earth of him! He's not fit to live!"' (Acts 22:21-22). Such prejudice and hostility are not only inspired by the devil, but are directed against the highest and noblest purpose of God, the salvation of a human soul.

> The fastest way to 'heap up ... sins to the limit' is to oppose the gospel.

The fastest way to 'heap up ... sins to the limit' is to oppose the gospel. By persecuting the prophets who 'predicted the sufferings of Christ and the glories that would follow' (1 Peter 1:11), by killing Jesus, who fulfilled the prophets, and by driving out the apostles, who pointed back to the cross, the Jews filled up to the brim the measure of their iniquities. Their sin had reached its fullness and thus they had sealed their own destruction.

Their extreme evil had filled the cup of God's wrath,

which stood ready to pour out on them many woes for rejecting Christ.

Let us never forget that God is a God of wrath. Jonathan Edwards in his famous sermon *Sinners in the hands of an angry God*, cried, 'O sinner! Consider the fearful danger you are in: it is a great furnace of wrath, a wide and bottomless pit, full of the fire of wrath, that you are held over in the hand of that God, whose wrath is provoked and incensed as much against you, as against many of the damned in hell. You hang by a slender thread, with the flames of divine wrath flashing about it, and ready every moment to singe it, and burn it asunder; and you have no interest in any Mediator, and nothing to lay hold of to save yourself, nothing to keep off the flames of wrath, nothing of your own, nothing that you ever have done, nothing that you can do, to induce God to spare you one moment.'

How shall we escape the just punishment of God, asks the apostle, if we ignore or oppose the 'great salvation' of God? 'If we deliberately keep on sinning after we have received the knowledge of the truth, no sacrifice for sins is left, but only a fearful expectation of judgement and of raging fire that will consume the enemies of God' (Heb. 10:26-27).

For further study ▶

FOR FURTHER STUDY

1. Read Psalm 19:7-11 again. Give several reasons why every Christian should read the Bible. Why do some Christians find it difficult to read the Scriptures? Suggest some practical 'helps' that might make Bible reading more enjoyable and effective.

2. Christians have been persecuted in every generation and treated in the most appalling manner. Why do some people react so aggressively to Jesus Christ? Read Acts 7:51-8:1 and try to understand why Stephen was stoned to death.

3. In Matthew 5:11-12 Jesus says we are 'blessed' when we are insulted and persecuted and that we should 'rejoice and be glad'. How is it possible to 'rejoice' when we are threatened and ill-treated by those who hate Christ?

TO THINK ABOUT AND DISCUSS

1. By today's standards Paul would be accused of anti-Semitism. Would this accusation be just? Discuss God's attitude to the Jews in the light of Romans 11.

2. Have you ever been insulted or abused because of your faith? If you have, how did you react?

3. There are many Christians suffering for their faith in the world today. Mention any individual or group that you know of and then spend some time in prayer for them.

6 Paul's love for the Thessalonians

(2:17-20)

Paul is continuing to answer his critics. In reply to their accusations that he has deserted the Thessalonians and has no intention of returning to those he has deceived, he makes a passionate defence and expresses a deep and genuine yearning to see them again.

A longing to return (v. 17)

So great was his love for the Thessalonians that he talks of being 'torn away' from them. This is a strong term to use and it means to be 'orphaned' or 'bereaved'. It is as if he was ripped from their grasp, although he assures them it was 'in person, not in thought'. Paul, along with Silas and Timothy, felt bereft of their loved ones and extremely anxious for a reunion, which is why they write, 'out of our intense longing we made every effort to see you'.

Stopped in their tracks (v. 18)

All the missionaries had a deep longing to see the Thessalonians again, and they tried repeatedly to return, especially Paul, 'but Satan stopped us'. The word 'stopped' means 'to dig a trench or to blow up the road in front of the enemy to hinder their advance'. The precise details of how Satan stopped them are not given, but what is clear is that Satan within certain limits is able to influence the affairs of men and retard the progress of the gospel.

However, it must not be forgotten that God's plans cannot be thwarted and through the wickedness of men and the evil schemes of the devil, God works out his eternal purpose. Paul reminded the Ephesians that God 'works out everything in conformity with the purpose of his will' (1:11). At times we may assume that evildoers and the devil have the upper hand, but it is a wrong and purely earthly assumption to make. If we are ever

> The Son of God was insulted and falsely accused, conspired against by Herod and Pontius Pilate, and finally murdered by the people he had come to save. On the surface it looked as though Satan had won a great victory, but it is clear that the enemies of the gospel only did what God's 'power and will had decided beforehand should happen' (Acts 4:28). God's purpose always prevails.

despondent about the state of the world, or confused about what is happening in our own lives, we must return to the truth of God's word, where it is emphatically stated, 'He does as he pleases with the powers of heaven and the peoples of the earth. No one can hold back his hand or say to him: "What have you done?"' (Dan. 4:35).

The Son of God was insulted and falsely accused, conspired against by Herod and Pontius Pilate, and finally murdered by the people he had come to save. On the surface it looked as though Satan had won a great victory, but it is clear that the enemies of the gospel only did what God's 'power and will had decided beforehand should happen' (Acts 4:28). God's purpose always prevails.

Their crown of glory (vv. 19-20)

By using expressions of endeared affection and of the highest estimation, Paul assures the Thessalonians that they mean everything to him. Just as a father dotes over his beloved child, so Paul glories in what God has done in the Thessalonians through his ministry. It is similar to when Jesus was baptised and the Father declared to the watching world, 'This is my Son, whom I love; with him I am well pleased' (Matt. 3:17). The Father was so proud of his Son that he announced his complete satisfaction with Jesus to all those who were prepared to listen.

At God's coming, the missionaries will experience the realization of their 'hope', supreme 'joy', and the 'glory'-wreath of victory. The word 'comes' either points to a state visit by a sovereign, whose arrival was marked by the presentation of an appropriate gift, or to the contributions that were collected for a crown of gold that was presented to a king at his coming. The Thessalonians are the crown, which the apostles will present to Christ when he returns to usher in the new age.

Paul again expresses the strength of his feelings for the Thessalonians when he says, 'you are our glory and joy'. The Thessalonians are the reason why the missionaries are glorifying in the Lord with great jubilation.

FOR FURTHER STUDY

1. Paul and his colleagues had a deep and genuine love for the Thessalonians. How did Jesus show his love for his disciples? Read John 21:15-25. What lesson was Jesus teaching Peter?
2. The devil is a foe that will do all he can to destroy our faith and to interrupt our spiritual progress. He prowls around like a roaring lion looking for someone to devour. Read Ephesians 6:10-18. How can we use each part of God's armour in our daily lives to take our stand against the devil's schemes?

TO THINK ABOUT AND DISCUSS

1. Who is your glory and joy?
2. What should our attitude be to the second coming? What is your opinion of some Christians who seem obsessed with the return of Christ? Can we be 'too heavenly minded to be any earthly good'?
3. Discuss how the second coming of Christ should affect our everyday behaviour.

7 Faith and persecution

(3:1-5)

Paul is unable to visit the Thessalonians himself, but because he is deeply concerned about them and is eager to learn about their spiritual wellbeing, he sends Timothy back to find out if they are standing firm in the faith.

Timothy (vv. 1-3a)

When Paul was in Athens, a city full of idols, he sent for Silas and Timothy. It appears that Silas was unable to make the journey immediately and so Timothy travelled on his own. Paul was delighted to see his 'brother and God's fellow-worker', who was useful to him in the gospel work. However, he was more concerned for the Thessalonians than for himself and was prepared to endure separation from Timothy if it benefited his friends in Macedonia. The phrase 'when we could stand it no longer' underlines the strength of Paul's feelings for the Thessalonians.

Paul sets an example for all ministers of the gospel and indeed all Christians, that we should be more concerned with the spiritual health of others than with our own comforts and desires. We are to look not only to our own interests, but also to the interests of others (Phil. 2:4).

> Paul sets an example for all ministers of the gospel and indeed all Christians, that we should be more concerned with the spiritual health of others than with our own comforts and desires.

When Jesus was being led to the place of execution, he turned to some women who 'mourned and wailed for him' and said to them, 'Daughters of Jerusalem, do not weep for me; weep for yourselves and for your children... For if men do these things when the tree is green, what will happen when it is dry?' (Luke 23:28-31). Even though he was about to be 'pierced for our transgressions' and 'crushed for our iniquities' (Isa. 53:5), he was prepared to counsel the broken-hearted. On the cross, during a time of unimaginable suffering, when he saw his mother and John the disciple standing near by, he spoke first to Mary, saying, 'Dear woman, here is your son', and then to the disciple, 'Here is your mother' (John 19:26-27). The Lamb of God, in the hour of his greatest need, was reaching out to others. In our time of suffering, may we learn to love our neighbours.

Timothy's credentials

Paul regarded Timothy as a 'brother' in Christ and therefore a member of God's household, and also 'God's fellow-worker in spreading the gospel of Christ', which was high praise and a strong recommendation to the churches and other believers. The gospel of Christ was the sphere in which Timothy worked. He was a preacher of the glad tidings of salvation. With Paul's backing, the Thessalonians would be happy to receive him and to listen to the word of life from his lips.

The purpose of Timothy's visit

Timothy was sent back to Thessalonica in order to 'strengthen and encourage' the believers in their new faith. Knowing that they were enduring persecution and that the enemy of souls was trying to undermine their stand for the truth, his purpose was not simply to learn about their progress in difficult times, but to urge them to remain steadfast in their obedience to Christ. Young Christians need to be nurtured and continually encouraged. They are like tender plants that can be easily trodden underfoot by the heavy boots of persecution. They need the advice and support of mature Christians, especially if their faith is being tested.

Paul did not want anyone to be 'unsettled by these trials'. He knew all too well that the enemies of Christ would be sowing seeds of doubt in their minds about the truth of the gospel, slandering the three missionaries, and urging them to return to the 'tried and trusted' lifestyle of idolatry. He knew the very real danger that those who are oppressed might be beguiled. He wanted no one to waver or be shaken by the difficulties they were encountering and he hoped Timothy would be like a wall of protection against the fiery darts of the evil one.

The devil is a real and deadly foe and the Christian needs to be self-controlled and alert at all times. Our enemy has many disguises and he pretends to be working for our good and happiness. He comes to us masquerading as an angel of light in an attempt to draw us back into darkness. We must stand firm, clothed in the full armour of God, crying out to our Saviour for the strength to resist his subtle attacks.

Persecuted for the faith (vv. 3b-5)

Paul tries to allay the fears of the Thessalonians about their troubles.

Destined

The problems they were encountering were not accidental, nor should they be surprised by them, for God had determined them. They were not caused simply by the wrath and malice of their enemies, but by God's appointment. We do not go looking for trouble as Christians, but it is a consequence of our faith and therefore we cannot avoid it. Paul had struggled through all sorts of persecutions and the Thessalonians were now experiencing the same treatment from those who were anti-Christ. When Paul wrote to Timothy he said, 'Everyone who wants to live a godly life in Christ Jesus will be persecuted' (2 Tim. 3:12). So if we are living wholeheartedly for Jesus Christ, we should expect persecution.

Prophesied

Not only were the Thessalonians 'destined' for trials, but the missionaries, when in Thessalonica, kept telling them that they would be persecuted. It was a certainty; therefore they should not be shaken by what was happening. Paul was never a flatterer; he always spoke the truth, even if it did not tickle the ears of his listeners. When Paul and Barnabas returned to Lystra, Iconium and Antioch, they strengthened the disciples and encouraged them to remain true to the faith, saying, 'We must go through many hardships to enter the kingdom of God' (Acts 14:22). Persecution is no strange thing, and to be forewarned is to be forearmed.

Fulfilled

The predicted persecutions came about in accordance with the will of God and therefore they must not upset the Thessalonians. In fact, they should have the opposite effect and strengthen their faith and cause them to rejoice that they have been counted worthy to suffer for the name of Christ. All too often we moan and groan in our afflictions instead of seeing them from a biblical point of view.

Many saints in previous generations regarded suffering as a 'gift from God'. They saw it as an instrument that moulded them into the image of Christ and caused them to worship with a deeper and more sincere faith.

One of these suffering saints was Charles Spurgeon, who once said, 'At the close of a dark and gloomy day, I lay resting on my couch as the deeper night drew on; and though all was bright within my cosy room, some of the external darkness seemed to have entered my soul and obscured its spiritual vision. In sorrow of heart I asked, "Why does my Lord deal thus with his child? Why does he permit lingering weakness to hinder the sweet service I long to render to his poor servants?" For a while silence reigned in the little room, broken only by the crackling of the oak log burning in the fireplace. Suddenly I heard a sweet soft sound, a little clear musical note like the tender trill of a robin beneath my window. "What can it be? Surely no bird is singing out there at this time of the year and night."

'My friend exclaimed, "It comes from the log on the fire!"

'The fire was letting loose the imprisoned music from the old oak's inmost heart! Perchance he had garnered up this song in the days when all was well with him, when birds twittered merrily on his branches, and the soft sunlight flecked his tender leaves with gold. Ah, thought I, when the fire of affliction draws songs of praise from us then indeed we are purified and our God is glorified. As I mused, the fire burned and my soul found sweet comfort in the parable so strangely set forth before me. Singing in the fire! Yes, God helping us, if that is the only way to get harmony out of these hard apathetic hearts, let the furnace be heated seven times hotter than before.'

Satan had stopped Paul from visiting them, so in his desperate need to find out about their faith, he had sent Timothy to them. Once again he says, 'when I could stand it no longer', which expresses his anxiety to know how the Thessalonians were faring under trials. Paul makes it clear that the Christian life is pre-eminently a life of faith. He was more concerned about their faith than their prosperity or physical wellbeing.

He was afraid that 'in some way the tempter might have tempted you and our efforts might have been useless'. He thought they might have been tempted to abandon the faith and return to their old way of life, and unless he sent Timothy he had no way of finding out.

The devil's main object is to stop people from believing, but when he fails his next aim is to destroy their faith. He may use intellectual arguments to cause us to doubt the Bible and its message; he may use ridicule and verbal abuse to shame us into turning from Christ; he may tempt us into sin and then declare that God has abandoned us because of our unfaithfulness; or he may appear as an angel of light to persuade us that there is a better way. But whatever his method, true faith withstands persecution and deception.

If the Thessalonians had abandoned their faith, Paul and the other apostles would have laboured for nothing.

For further study ▶

FOR FURTHER STUDY

1. Jesus often told his disciples that they would be persecuted. Read Matthew 10:17-23; 24:4-13 and John 16:1-4. Why do some unbelievers persecute Christians for their faith? Why does God allow persecution to occur?
2. The devil is very subtle and he uses every opportunity to hinder the gospel and to destroy its fruit. What does the Bible tell us to do when we are under spiritual attack? Read Job chapters 1 and 2. What were some of the temptations that Job had to resist?

TO THINK ABOUT AND DISCUSS

1. Some Christians think they see the devil in almost everything that happens, whereas other Christians hardly recognize him at all. How can we distinguish between the specific attacks of the devil and the problems that occur simply because we live in a fallen world?
2. 1 Corinthians 10:13 is an encouraging verse. What does it mean? Can you remember a situation when you experienced the reality of this verse?
3. Was Paul right to indicate that the Christian life is pre-eminently a life of faith? Give reasons for your answer.

8 Good news

(3:6-10)

All Paul's anxiety for the Thessalonians disappeared when Timothy returned and gave such an encouraging report of their faith. Paul was so thrilled with the news that he wrote to them immediately. By this time Silas had travelled from Berea and the three men were reunited.

Timothy's report (v. 6)

Paul was delighted with what Timothy had to say. The believers in Thessalonica had not forsaken the gospel or been shaken by the persecution they were enduring. Their faith in God and love for others, which is the sum total of godliness, were growing and giving evidence of the power of the gospel. There is a slight play on words here as Paul in effect says, 'Timothy has just brought good news about your steadfastness to the good news of the gospel.'

Genuine faith is not destroyed by trials but proved genuine and results in 'praise, glory and honour when Jesus Christ is revealed' (1 Peter 1:7). Just as dross is burnt away when gold passes through the fire, so unbelief is purged when believers pass through the fires of affliction. The faith of the Thessalonians, rather than being crushed by persecution, shone all the more brightly through the darkness that was trying to extinguish it.

Paul was also delighted because the Thessalonians had not turned against him or grown cold in their affection from listening to the slander and insinuations that abounded. On the contrary, they had 'pleasant memories' of the missionaries and had not forgotten the founder of the church. Indeed, they were as eager to see the apostles as the apostles were to see them. There was a mutual longing, which caused Paul to rejoice.

Paul's response (3:7-10)

Paul was genuinely thrilled with the news he received about their commitment to Christ, and it revitalized his spirit.

Encouraged

Timothy's report had brought Paul much-needed encouragement and confirmed to him that his work among the Thessalonians had not been in vain. He therefore rose above his present 'distress and persecution' in Corinth and continued his mission there with renewed zeal. Paul was prepared to endure anything for the sake of the gospel as long as his ministry bore fruit.

Paul had specifically asked Timothy to find out about the

faith of the Thessalonians. When he heard about the love they were showing for others and the love they expressed for him personally, he knew that their faith had stood the test of time. Love for Christ and love for others spring from faith in God. In this case, absence, as well as distress and persecution, had made the heart grow fonder.

> Genuine faith is not destroyed by trials but proved genuine and results in 'praise, glory and honour when Jesus Christ is revealed' (1 Peter 1:7).

There is nothing that spurs us on more than seeing people converted and growing in their faith. It is an encouragement that we all need. And when those who have been converted through our instrumentality are particularly affectionate towards us, it is a double honour that makes us rejoice all the more in the Lord's goodness to us.

Revitalized

Paul was so thrilled with Timothy's report that he made a statement of profound and overpowering emotion: 'Now we really live, since you are standing firm in the Lord.' He was given a new lease of life to work for God. His heart was on fire for the Lord and he was filled with a tender affection for the Thessalonians, since they were rooted and established in Christ, loving and serving him with all their hearts, and refusing to be intimidated by threats and persecution. His own confidence in the gospel was strengthened by this report and he realized afresh that God was working in the lives of the believers 'to will and to act according to his good purpose' (Phil. 2:13).

It might be interesting to ask what Paul's response would have been if Timothy had told him that the Thessalonians had forsaken the Lord and did not want to see him again. We can imagine a profound disappointment in Paul's heart and yet a steely determination to revisit them to see why they had turned their backs on Christ. Paul was not a man to give up without a fight. He would have done his utmost to convince them to return to the shepherd of their souls, and prayed without ceasing for their restoration, not in a spirit of rejoicing and gratitude, but from a burden that the devil had tripped them up in the race they were running.

> Whenever we are encouraged, our hearts should automatically turn to God in thanksgiving and praise.

If we find that new believers are wavering in their faith and rejecting the truth, we must not give up on them. Instead, we must pray more fervently and work harder to remind them of the 'glorious gospel of the blessed God' (1 Tim. 1:11). In our battle for their souls we must remember we do not struggle 'against flesh and blood, but against the rulers, against the authorities, against the powers of this dark world and against the spiritual forces of evil in the heavenly realms' (Eph. 6:12); and that the Captain of our salvation possesses 'all authority in heaven and on earth' (Matt. 28:18). We can therefore fight with confidence.

Joyful

Paul's first reaction to Timothy's report was to give thanks to God, from whom every good and perfect gift comes. In fact, he was so full of joy that he could never thank God enough for their steadfast faith. It is almost as if he felt grieved that he could not give God the praise he deserved for keeping his dear friends safe from the attacks of their enemies.

Whenever we are encouraged, our hearts should automatically turn to God in thanksgiving and praise. We must be like Paul who was flooded with gratitude. How easy it is to grumble when things go wrong or to point an accusing finger at others! When our plans do not succeed, we should quietly trust in God who in all things 'works for the good of those who love him, who have been called according to his purpose' (Rom. 8:28). A complaining Christian is really a contradiction. On the one hand, he says he submits to an almighty God, who 'does as he pleases with the powers of heaven and the peoples of the earth' (Dan. 4:35), while on the other hand, he denies his faith by complaining about the circumstances that God has brought into his life.

One day a man was invited to eat dinner with an old Indian, a highly respected man in the community. They walked to the hotel together. As soon as the food was served at the table, the man began to eat, but the Indian paused, bowed his head and gave thanks to God for the food. A little while later he said to the man, 'Do you know what a man reminds me of who sits down at the table and eats the food that God gives him without thanking God for it?'

'No,' said the man abruptly as he continued to eat. He

obviously did not care to talk about such matters.

'Well,' said the Indian, 'the man who sits down at the table and eats the food that God gives him without thanking God for it, reminds me a good deal of the pig under a chestnut tree eating chestnuts, and doesn't so much as look up to see where the chestnuts come from.'

Whenever something good happens, we must look up and give praise and thanksgiving to our gracious and merciful God. Later in the epistle Paul says, 'Be joyful always' and 'give thanks in all circumstances' (5:16, 18). That should be our attitude.

Prayerful

By night and by day Paul and his companions prayed 'most earnestly' that God would open the way for them to visit Thessalonica again. It seems that their present joy increased their desire to return to see their friends again.

Paul's thanksgiving was accompanied by prayer because he wanted to 'supply what is lacking' in their faith. It was similar to his desire for the Roman Christians: 'I long to see you so that I may impart to you some spiritual gift to make you strong' (Rom. 1:11). He knew they were still babes in Christ and needed further instruction in the things of God in order to reach a more perfect obedience to the principles they had already been taught. Paul wanted to sort out the confusion they were experiencing concerning Christ's second coming, and to encourage them to abound in love more and more.

In order to underline the importance of prayer, Hudson Taylor related the following anecdote about a young man who had been called to the foreign field. He had not been in the habit of preaching, but he knew how to prevail with God in prayer. Going one day to a friend, he said, 'I don't see how God can use me on the field; I have no special talent.'

His friend replied, 'My brother, God wants men on the field who can pray. There are too many preachers now and too few prayers.'

The young man became a missionary. In his room in the early dawn, a voice was heard weeping and pleading for souls. All through the day, the closed door and the hush that prevailed made you feel like walking softly, for a soul was wrestling with God. To his home hungry souls would flock, drawn by an irresistible power. In the morning hours some would call and cry, 'I have gone by your home and have longed to come in. Will you tell me how I can be saved?' From some distant place another would call, saying, 'I heard you would tell us here how we might find heart-rest.'

Prayer and thanksgiving are the two legs on which a Christian must walk in his relationship with God. We can never pray enough. We can never give thanks enough. There is always something or someone to pray about, and there is always something or someone to give thanks for. Paul repeats this message to the Philippians: 'Rejoice in the Lord always. I will say it again: Rejoice! Let your gentleness be evident to all. The Lord is near. Do not be anxious about anything, but in everything, by prayer and petition, with thanksgiving, present your requests to God. And the peace of God, which transcends all understanding, will guard your hearts and your minds in Christ Jesus' (Phil. 4:4-7).

FOR FURTHER STUDY

1. Paul rejoiced because the Thessalonians were standing firm in the faith. Read Hebrews 11. What is faith? Why is faith so important to the Christian? Read verses 32-39 again. Why are Christians prepared to be tortured, flogged and put in prison for their faith?

2. If God works out everything in conformity with the purpose of his will, what is the point of praying?

TO THINK ABOUT AND DISCUSS

1. Name some of the blessings for which you can thank God.

2. In the Psalms it often tells us to give thanks to the LORD, for he is good. What is the difference between thanking God for his blessings and thanking him for his goodness?

3. Think about your own prayer life. What are some of the difficulties you experience in prayer? How can your prayer life be improved?

4. Read Matthew 6:5-15 and then discuss the prayer life of Jesus in the light of what he says in that passage.

9 A remarkable petition

(3:11-13)

This remarkable petition is more a devout utterance than a prayer, for prayer is always directed to God. Paul wants his prayers of verse 10 to be fulfilled.

May the Lord Jesus clear the way (v. 11)

Whatever Paul did or said he always acknowledged God. Here he is stressing the unity of the Father and the Son in their divinity and in hearing and answering prayer. The Father and Son are never at cross-purposes. There is never any disagreement between them. The Father is not more loving than the Son and the Son is not more willing to grant our petitions than the Father, for both are indivisibly and perfectly one.

Paul's desire is that 'our God and Father himself and our Lord Jesus' would go before him to make a straight and level path for him to revisit the Thessalonians by removing all the obstacles that Satan had erected to prevent such a reunion. It is not clear if God answered in the way Paul wanted, but Acts 20:1-4 suggests that Paul did return. Again we see Paul's dependence on God and his love for the Thessalonians.

May the Lord Jesus make your love increase (v. 12)

Whether or not Paul was permitted by God to return to Thessalonica, he nevertheless expresses his desire for them. He not only wants them to grow in the grace of love for other Christians, for non-believers, and even for their persecutors, but he wants that love to 'overflow'. They should be so full of love for others that they cannot contain it. It must seep out of every part of their lives and be touching those with whom they come into contact.

Love in action is the outward evidence and expression of a living faith. James asks, 'What good is it, my brothers, if a man claims to have faith but has no deeds? Can such faith save him? Suppose a brother or sister is without clothes and daily food. If one of you says to him, "Go, I wish you well; keep warm and well fed," but does nothing about his physical needs, what good is it? In the same way, faith by itself, if it is not accompanied by action, is dead.

'But someone will say, "You have faith; I have deeds."

'Show me your faith without deeds, and I will show you my faith by what I do' (James 2:14-18).

Jesus made it abundantly clear that we are to love our enemies and to pray for those who persecute us. In our own strength such commands are impossible to obey, but Paul and his colleagues knew that the Lord is the source of love, which is why they pointed to themselves as a demonstration of divine love. The Thessalonians had seen the love that the

Lord produces in action in the lives of the three missionaries, and therefore they had personal examples to follow.

Many years ago the *Princess Alice* collided with another boat in dense fog on the River Thames and about 600 people drowned in the dark waters. Nearby two ferrymen were mooring their boats for the night. Both heard the noise of the collision and the screams of the stranded but they reacted differently. The first ferryman said to himself, 'I am tired after a long hard day and I am going home; no one will see me in the fog. It will be an impossible task to save anyone.' At the coroner's inquest the ferryman was asked, 'Did you hear the cries?'

> They should be so full of love for others that they cannot contain it. It must seep out of every part of their lives and be touching those with whom they come into contact.

'Yes, sir.'

'What did you do?'

'Nothing, sir.'

'Are you an Englishman? Aren't you ashamed?'

'Sir, the shame will never leave me till I die.'

The second ferryman, as soon as he heard the cries for help, jumped back into his boat and rowed as hard as he could towards the wreck. He found numerous survivors floundering in the water, and crammed as many women and children as he could into his boat. When it became too dangerous for him to take anyone else he rowed to shore with the cry, 'O God, for a bigger boat!'

Are we more like the first or second ferryman? When we hear cries for help, do we make excuses as to why we cannot assist, or do we jump into our boat and row to the rescue? Love is very practical, and yet it is so easy to find reasons not to exercise practical love when others are in need.

There are times when we must stop and examine our lives in the light of the Scriptures and ask ourselves some poignant questions. Is our faith expressed in our love for others? Do we love with actions and in truth as the apostle John commands? In what ways do we love our fellow believers? Would our non-Christian neighbours or work colleagues say that our lives are characterized by love? How do we respond if someone criticizes our faith? How do we demonstrate the love of God to those people who are openly antagonistic towards us? It is possible to march on in the Christian life without ever closely inspecting our lives to see if they measure up to the word of God.

> In what ways do we love our fellow believers? Would our non-Christian neighbours or work colleagues say that our lives are characterized by love?

May the Lord Jesus strengthen your hearts (v. 13)

The purpose of love is to strengthen the inward aims and desires of our hearts so that on the day of God's judgement we might be found in a blameless state of holiness. The effect of increasing and abounding love is to separate us from sin and to establish us more firmly in the way of righteousness, which is what Paul desired for the Thessalonians.

While the act of perfecting us is God's work, it nevertheless needs our cooperation: 'Continue to work out your salvation with fear and trembling, for it is God who works in you to will and to act according to his good purpose,' said Paul to the Philippians (Phil. 2:12-13). We must never contradict our profession of faith by our behaviour or allow selfish lusts to overcome selfless love.

Paul encourages and comforts the believers by reminding them that the Lord Jesus will certainly come again in glory 'with all his holy ones'. These holy ones are not angels but holy men and women who have died in the Lord. They will be the first to rise from the dead, and Jesus will bring them with him when he returns to his people on earth. Not one will be left behind.

The Thessalonians must look beyond the trials and tribulations they are enduring to the great day of Christ's return when all their troubles will be overcome and when they will be perfectly united with their Saviour for ever. Nothing comforts us more in our distresses than the knowledge of Christ's second advent. It will be a day of great rejoicing and victory, when all we have strived to achieve is accomplished. Let us lift up our heads, for our redemption draws near.

For further study ▶

FOR FURTHER STUDY

1. Love is one of the main themes of the Bible and one of the characteristics of God. Read Matthew 5:43-48 and explain in practical terms how we can love our enemies. In what ways does God love his enemies?
2. In Matthew 5:48 Jesus tells his disciples to 'be perfect, therefore, as your heavenly Father is perfect'. Is that a reasonable command? Is it possible to be as perfect as God? What does Jesus mean?
3. Read Genesis 6:5-22. Why is Noah described as 'righteous' and 'blameless among the people of his time'? What was different about his life? In what ways do our lives differ from our non-Christian friends' lives?

TO THINK ABOUT AND DISCUSS

1. The Bible makes it clear that Jesus is God. What arguments would you use to convince a friend or colleague of the deity of Christ?
2. Discuss the various views Christians hold on the second coming of Christ.
3. In what ways should the reality of the second coming affect our daily lives?
4. Paul used his own life as an example for others to follow. In what areas can we hold up our lives to be imitated?

10 Living to please God

(4:1-8)

This section opens a more practical part of the letter in which Paul exhorts the Thessalonians to live sanctified lives at all times and before all people. His instructions are based on the report he had received from Timothy.

Introduction (v. 1)

By tactfully calling them 'brothers', Paul expresses his confidence not only in their salvation, but also in their willingness to hear and obey the instructions he is passing on. What he is saying is nothing new, for he had told them the same things when in Thessalonica, so they cannot plead ignorance as an excuse.

The gospel of Jesus Christ does not simply teach us what to believe, but it regulates our behaviour and shows us 'how to live in order to please God'. It directs our lives into holiness and enables us to 'walk the talk'. This in turn pleases God.

The Thessalonians were living holy lives, but Paul did not

want then to rest on their laurels so he urges them 'in the Lord Jesus to do this more and more'. Paul is driving them on to overflow with godly living. They must make it their constant aim to live more and more in obedience to the Lord's commands. Paul says 'in the Lord Jesus' to emphasize that his instructions come by virtue of his union with the Lord, whom he represents and whose Spirit inspires him.

The purpose of believers is to please God in all things. We are to abound in the work of faith and to live lives that are worthy of the calling we have received. We are to produce fruit in keeping with repentance and to honour God in private and in public. The Christian life is a bit like climbing a ladder. The higher we climb the more we are transformed into the image of God.

Paul's authority (v. 2)

The word 'instructions' is a military term and is used strictly of commands given by someone in authority to an inferior, who must carry them out. These instructions, imparted to the Thessalonians during the missionaries' visit, were given 'by the authority of the Lord Jesus'. They were Christ's commands. Such a comment added weight to Paul's exhortation and reminded the Thessalonians that Paul was Christ's minister proclaiming Christ's will; therefore, whoever rejects his 'instructions' rejects God.

Avoid sexual immorality (vv. 3-8)

Paul makes it explicit that it is God's will for them to be 'holy' or 'sanctified'. Sanctification is both a gift and a demand, and those who follow Christ must turn from all that is impure and polluted, renounce the fleshly desires of the sinful nature, and honour God with their bodies. God has called us to be holy in all that we do, say and think. Only when we follow the path of holiness will we be transformed into Christ's likeness.

Paul mentions three specific ways in which Christians can live sanctified lives, and they are all relating to the same subject:

'AVOID SEXUAL IMMORALITY.' Just as the Thessalonians had to reject every form of sexual vice that was prevalent in Greek society, so every Christian must flee from every temptation to relapse into disgraceful practices. Whether one is married or unmarried, sexual immorality, in every shape or form, must be avoided.

'LEARN TO CONTROL YOUR OWN BODY.' It is God's will for us to be self-controlled in sexual matters. Each man must learn to live with his own wife, and each woman must learn to live with her own husband, and fornication is to be shunned as contrary to God's holy will. Instead of indulging in a life of sin and shame, we should behave 'in a way that is holy and honourable' in the sight of God. The heathen, from their ignorance of God, sink into 'passionate lust', a lifestyle that is utterly opposed to a saving knowledge of God. For a Christian to follow such shameful conduct is incomprehensible, for it is to exchange light for darkness, liberty for bondage, and life for death. It makes no sense for a Christian, who has crucified the flesh with its evil affections and lusts, to resurrect that flesh by gratifying its sinful cravings.

'NO ONE SHOULD WRONG HIS BROTHER.' In the matter of

sexual immorality no one should violate his neighbour's rights by committing adultery with his wife. To steal another man's wife or daughter for sexual pleasure is to rob him of what rightfully belongs to him. Adultery is not only a sin against God, but a sin against a fellow human being.

Knowing the temptations to licentiousness that everywhere abound, Paul had already warned the Thessalonians that the Lord would 'punish men for all such sins'. God avenges sexual sin, especially when someone takes another man's wife and commits adultery with her in the passion of lust. All who refuse to tread the path of sanctification will be dealt with severely by the Lord Jesus on the Day of Judgement, if not before. The writer to the Hebrews says, 'Marriage should be honoured by all, and the marriage bed kept pure, for God will judge the adulterer and all the sexually immoral' (Heb. 13:4).

> All who refuse to tread the path of sanctification will be dealt with severely by the Lord Jesus on the Day of Judgement.

In our sex-mad society of the twenty-first century, where morals are frowned upon and immorality is common place, the Christian must stand strong and with his life acknowledge that he has been called out of impurity to 'live a holy life'. It is inconceivable that a holy God should call us to any kind of uncleanness; instead, his commands are unambiguous: 'As obedient children, do not conform to the evil desires you had when you lived in ignorance. But just as he who called you is holy, so be holy in all you do; for it is written: "Be holy, because I am holy"' (1 Peter 1:14-16). Holiness should be the element in which a Christian daily moves.

A Christian who shows contempt for God's law is showing contempt for God himself, who gives us his Holy Spirit. The special characteristic of the Holy Spirit, who lives in every believer, is holiness. Therefore, to live in an unholy manner while receiving the gift of the Holy Spirit is both insulting and grievous to God. To walk in such a way is to move him to withdraw from us.

Every Christian should be filled with the Holy Spirit, who arms us against immorality and helps us to put to death the acts of the sinful nature. 'For if you live according to the sinful nature, you will die; but if by the Spirit you put to death the misdeeds of the body, you will live' (Rom. 8:13).

For further study ▶

FOR FURTHER STUDY

1. What does the word 'holiness' mean? Give examples of holiness in the life and teaching of Jesus.
2. Paul has a great deal to say about sexual immorality. Read 1 Corinthians 5. What guidelines are laid down on how we should deal with a Christian who is sexually immoral? What does it mean to hand a man over to Satan? Why does Paul tell the Corinthians to 'expel the wicked man from among you'?
3. Read 1 Corinthians 6:12-20. What does Paul mean when he says 'our bodies are members of Christ himself'? How do we honour God with our bodies?

TO THINK ABOUT AND DISCUSS

1. Apart from living a holy life, how else can we please the Lord?
2. Our society is flooded with images that are designed to entice and seduce. Newspapers and magazines exploit the female body, advertisements are often suggestive and even films for young people are regarded as incomplete without a sex scene. How can Christians protect themselves from the filth that abounds in society? Suggest some ways that parents can control what their children watch on TV and what they do in their spare time.
3. What safeguards should a Christian use when talking to a person of the opposite sex?

11 Love and ambition

(4:9-12)

Paul is pleased with the way the Thessalonians are demonstrating their faith and by tactfully appreciating their behaviour he is preparing the ground for various exhortations.

Brotherly love (vv. 9-10)

There is nothing more important in the Christian's life than love. It is the foundation of all other graces and should abound in all our service for Christ.

The 'brotherly love' that Paul mentions, according to classical Greek, is a love to brothers by birth, but in the New Testament it refers to the special love Christians have for one another because they are members of the same family and have the same Father. Paul does not think it is necessary to write to the Thessalonians about this grace, as it is so evident in their lives, for he knows they have been 'taught by God to love each other'. Although Paul spoke to them about love when he was in Thessalonica, it was God the Holy Spirit in them who taught them how to live in love. Everything good comes from God and our praise should therefore be directed to him.

Thessalonica was the natural centre of the Macedonian churches and the Christians there were using their influence to bless their brothers in the surrounding area. So effective was their witness that whoever came into contact with them throughout Macedonia was a recipient of the love of Christ. The Christian church should be as extensive as possible. Our love should reach beyond the boundaries of our immediate neighbourhood and into the lives of those we may never meet. The change that has taken place in our hearts because of God's grace should be proclaimed abroad through the example of our love.

> Our love should reach beyond the boundaries of our immediate neighbourhood and into the lives of those we may never meet. The change that has taken place in our hearts because of God's grace should be proclaimed abroad through the example of our love.

It may help us to remember what Archbishop Usher called the eleventh commandment. The archbishop was once wrecked off the coast of Ireland and being almost destitute of clothing, wandered to the house of a local clergyman, who was suspicious of his identity and cold towards him. After a few minutes of uncomfortable silence, the clergyman demanded, 'How many commandments are there?' fully expecting to uncover an impostor.

'I can at once satisfy you that I am not an impostor, as you think,' replied the archbishop, 'for there are eleven commandments.'

'No,' interrupted the clergyman, pleased that his suspicions had been well founded, 'there are only ten commandments. If you can tell me the eleventh commandment, I shall give you all you need.'

'Bring me a Bible.' Turning to John 13:34, he read, 'A new commandment I give unto you, that ye love one another; as I have loved you, that ye also love one another' (AV).

With that the clergyman was ready to help him in every way.

Paul did not want the Thessalonians to rest on their reputation so he urged them to keep moving forward in love. Perfection this side of heaven is never attained; there is always room for spiritual growth and progress, however mature we might be.

Ambition (vv. 11-12)

Today the voices in the world tell us that if we are to get anywhere in life, then we must be ambitious. This often means striving to reach the top of our profession and earning enough money so we can retire early and live a life of ease. Paul wants his readers to be ambitious in a different sense. 'Make it your ambition,' he says,

'TO LEAD A QUIET LIFE.' He is probably referring to those Christians who had become over-excited, perhaps even fanatical, about the second coming of Christ. Rather than being restless and impatient for Christ's return and placing an over-emphasis on it, he wants them to wait calmly and quietly for that great day. This is sound advice, for there are many today who can think and talk about little else. We must never be so preoccupied with Christ's return that it distracts us from fulfilling the great commission or from loving our neighbours. Our ambition should not be to interpret the signs of the times or to convince all and sundry that our views of the second coming are correct, but to 'lead a quiet life' that glorifies God and honours the gospel.

'TO MIND YOUR OWN BUSINESS.' It is likely that some of the Christians in Thessalonica had stopped working because they thought that Christ's return was imminent. With nothing to do, they had become busybodies, meddling in matters that did not concern them and interfering with the affairs of others, especially the church leaders from whom they wanted support. Idleness is an abuse of brotherly love: instead of supporting ourselves, we have to rely on others to meet our needs. There are two English proverbs worth remembering in this regard: 'Idleness is the parent of all vice' and 'No mill, no meal; an idle brain is the devil's workshop.'

'TO WORK WITH YOUR HANDS.' While in Thessalonica, Paul had set the Christians an example to follow by working hard to earn his keep. The best way to prepare for Christ's return is not to become a loafer in an ivory tower, but to be faithful in everyday duties and to work hard for the benefit of others.

The outcome of such a way of life will be to 'win the respect of outsiders'. Those who do not believe in Christ will respect the way we live and be more ready to spread a good report about Christianity. A great deal of harm is done to the gospel because fanatical Christians neglect their daily work because of some religious excitement. We should behave according to the Scriptures and so not prejudice our cause in the eyes of the world.

When we earn bread to eat it means we are 'not dependent on anybody'. Instead of looking to others to help us, we are ready and able to support the needy. The hard-working will live comfortably and lack nothing, whereas poverty will come on the lazy 'like a bandit and scarcity like an armed man' (Prov. 6:11). 'The sluggard craves and gets nothing, but the desires of the diligent are fully satisfied' (Prov. 13:4).

There is a poignant Hebrew legend about two brothers who lived on adjacent farms. One was the head of a large family; the other lived alone. One night the former lay awake and thought, 'My brother lives alone and he doesn't have the companionship of a wife and children to cheer his heart as I have. While he sleeps, I shall carry some of my sheaves into his field.'

At the same hour, the other brother lay awake and reasoned, 'My brother has a large family and his necessities are greater than mine. As he sleeps, I shall put some of my sheaves in his field.'

As the two brothers went out, carrying their sheaves, they met at the dividing line. There they embraced. Years later, the legend says, the temple of Jerusalem was built and on the very spot of the brothers' meeting, the altar of sacrifice stood.

It may only be a legend, but it makes the point that our ambition should be to love one another.

For further study ▶

FOR FURTHER STUDY

1. Read Luke 10:25-37. What is Jesus teaching in this parable and how can it be applied to our daily lives? What are some of the ways we can show Christian love to our families, colleagues and friends?
2. Read Luke 19:11-27. In this parable is Jesus exhorting us to work hard or is there another more important meaning?

TO THINK ABOUT AND DISCUSS

1. What are some of the ways brotherly love is expressed in your church? In what ways might your church grow in love?
2. Discuss the rights and wrongs of ambition in the life of a Christian.
3. The Bible tells us that a gossip separates close friends. What is gossip and how should we respond if someone gossips to us?
4. The second coming of Christ is an essential doctrine of the Christian faith and yet some preachers hardly ever mention it because they regard it as divisive. How can Christians with different views edify one another concerning the return of Christ?
5. What are some of the dangers of being preoccupied with the second coming?

12 The second coming of Christ

(4:13-18)

The apostle Paul begins a new section and endeavours to correct the error into which some of the Thessalonians had fallen. He focuses on the subject that was causing concern among the faint-hearted, many of whom were in despair over the friends and family members who had recently died.

The errors that troubled them probably included: the thought that only those believers who were alive at the second coming of Christ would be saved, that their dead brethren would not shine in glory, and that they would not receive new glorified bodies.

When L. Talbot left Australia years ago, he said to his mother, 'Mother, if God spares me, I shall come back to see you.'

For years she waited. Someone said to her, 'Mrs Talbot, what are you waiting for?'

She replied, 'My boy is in America and he's coming back soon.'

'Coming back? What do you mean? Surely you don't expect a personal, visible, actual coming!'

'Yes,' she said, 'that's the way he is coming.'

'Have you ever received any letters from him? Do you ever receive gifts? Well, that is what he meant—he is coming in all those things.'

'Why,' answered Talbot's mother, 'that isn't what he meant, for he said that he would come back!'

Some years later Talbot crossed the ocean and walked down the gangplank to greet his waiting mother with the words, 'Mother, here I am!'

So the second coming of Christ will be 'a personal, visible, actual coming'.

Do not be ignorant (v. 13)

Ignorance of the truth causes anxiety. Since the Thessalonians had heard and believed the gospel, some of their fellow Christians had died and they were concerned about their eternal safety. As a result they were in danger of grieving like pagans who have no hope of a bodily resurrection to eternal life. Paul contrasts the black despair of death that accompanies the mourning of pagans with the glorious Christian hope. In death, pagans embrace hopelessness, because as far as they are concerned death is the end and there is nothing beyond; whereas Christians, although they grieve over their departed loved ones, grieve in the hope of a better and more glorious future for them.

The hope of resurrection (v. 14)

The logical conclusion of the death and resurrection of Jesus is that all those who believe in him, whether dead or alive, will rise again to eternal life. The Thessalonians had to realize that not even death severs the union of a believer with Christ, which is the foundation of the Christian's hope: 'Christ has indeed been raised from the dead, the firstfruits of those who have fallen asleep' (1 Cor. 15:20).

If there is no resurrection, then Christians are to be pitied more than all men, for our faith is futile and we are still in our sins. But Christ has been raised and so in Christ all believers are made alive.

Paul goes further, for he says that not only will believers be resurrected, but 'God will bring with Jesus those who have fallen asleep in him'. The God who raised Jesus will raise the followers of Jesus. He will bring their souls from heaven to be united with their bodies; therefore, all believers can die in peace with the song of triumph on their lips:

'"Death has been swallowed up in victory."

'"Where, O death, is your victory?

'"Where, O death, is your sting?"

'The sting of death is sin, and the power of sin is the law.

> In death, pagans embrace hopelessness, because as far as they are concerned death is the end and there is nothing beyond; whereas Christians, although they grieve over their departed loved ones, grieve in the hope of a better and more glorious future for them.

But thanks be to God! He gives us the victory through our Lord Jesus Christ' (1 Cor. 15:54-57).

The coming of the Lord (vv. 15-16a)

'According to the Lord's own word' either refers to an unrecorded saying or a direct revelation given to Paul from the risen Lord Jesus. Paul compares the living and the dead and speaks as though the second coming could occur at any time, although in 2 Thessalonians 2:3 he says that the day of the Lord will not come 'until the rebellion occurs and the man of lawlessness is revealed, the man doomed to destruction'. He wants the Thessalonians to live as if the day is imminent; however, he does not say they will still be alive at Christ's coming.

Paul assures the Thessalonians that living believers will have no advantage over dead believers, for both the living and the dead in Christ will be gloriously joined in glory to the glorious Lord. In fact, the order seems to be that the souls of the redeemed who have died will leave heaven and be joined with their new bodies before the resurrection of the living.

There is no reason to grieve over the dead, for the Lord himself will descend from heaven:

'WITH A LOUD COMMAND.' The Lord will awaken the dead with an irresistible command as he returns to save those for whom he died. This is the shout of a king or conqueror as he leaves his palace with the expressed aim of setting the captives free. Just as Jesus gave life to the dead when he was on earth, so the voice of the Son of God will give life to the dead when he returns from heaven. Rather than this being a secret rapture, it will be an audible and visible advent. 'Look, he is coming with the clouds, and every eye will see him, even those who pierced him; and all the peoples of the earth will mourn because of him. So shall it be! Amen' (Rev. 1:7).

'WITH THE VOICE OF AN ARCHANGEL.' The archangel may or may not be Michael—the Bible does not say. Here is another signal for the dead in Christ to arise.

'WITH THE TRUMPET CALL OF GOD.' In the Old Testament the trumpet sounded to summon the people to meet with God and to signal deliverance from oppression; so the final trumpet will sound to gather the elect from the four corners of the earth to meet with their Saviour and to usher in for them an eternal deliverance from every sort of oppression.

The resurrection of the dead and living (vv. 16b-17)

If we live in Christ, we shall die in Christ, and if we die in Christ, we shall be raised with Christ when he returns. Although the transformation of the dead will precede the transformation of the living, both will be snatched up 'in the clouds', which is the space between heaven and earth. The words 'caught up' show the suddenness and swiftness of the rapture and can be compared with Acts 8:39, where 'the Spirit of the Lord suddenly took Philip away, and the eunuch did not see him again'.

All believers will be caught up in the clouds 'to meet the Lord in the air'. The word 'meet' refers to the welcome given to a newly arrived magistrate by the leading citizens who gladly hurry out to meet him and then escort him back to the city. After this meeting, the Lord will pass the final judgement on the devil and the wicked, which will be approved and applauded by all believers, who themselves will receive crowns of glory.

'And so we will be with the Lord for ever.' The believer's hope and joy are complete when he goes home to be with his Saviour. There is no greater blessing than to be with our Redeemer, to see him as he is in glory, to live with him for ever, to enjoy him eternally, to love him perfectly. Heaven is only heaven because Jesus Christ is there. When Jesus said to the dying thief, 'Today you will be with me in paradise', the most precious words were the words 'with me'. Oh, to be with Christ! No wonder Paul could say to the Philippians, 'For to me, to live is Christ and to die is gain ... I desire to depart and be with Christ, which is better by far' (1:21, 23). Paul did not want to die to escape a life of hardships and pain, but to be with his Lord and Saviour.

Encourage one another (v. 18)

Here is genuine encouragement that we can offer each other because there is a real hope of the resurrection of the dead. When our loved ones die in the Lord, we must not grieve excessively for we shall all meet again when the Lord returns.

FOR FURTHER STUDY

1. Did Old Testament believers have a hope of the resurrection from the dead? Support your answer with references from the Bible. Read Psalm 49 and contrast the fate of the wicked with the hope of the psalmist.
2. In Acts 1:11 the angels said to the men of Galilee, 'This same Jesus, who has been taken from you into heaven, will come back in the same way you have seen him go into heaven.' In what way is the second coming of Christ similar to Christ's ascension?
3. Read 1 Corinthians 15:35-58 and describe the resurrected body of believers. Why should the resurrection of the dead encourage us to give ourselves fully to the work of the Lord?

TO THINK ABOUT AND DISCUSS

1. Why does ignorance of biblical truth lead to anxiety and fear?
2. List all the things mentioned in Romans 8:35-39 that will not be able to separate us from the love of God that is in Christ Jesus our Lord, and then discuss them individually.
3. How can we encourage other believers in their faith?

13 Sons of the light

(5:1-11)

Paul is seeking to allay the fears of the Thessalonians, who probably thought they had to be alive at the second coming if they were to receive eternal life. That is why they were concerned about the date of Christ's return and were no doubt watching for 'signs' to see if it was imminent.

A thief in the night (vv. 1-3)

The Lord Jesus Christ will return to judge the living and the dead, but no one knows the date or time. Jesus told his disciples, 'No one knows about that day or hour, not even the angels in heaven, nor the Son, but only the Father' (Matt. 24:36). Instead of speculating about dates, our responsibility as Christians is to fulfil our duties and to serve the Lord with all our strength. In that way, we shall be prepared for Christ's return whenever he comes.

Paul had no need to write to the Thessalonians about 'times and dates' because the missionaries had already instructed them when in Macedonia. They knew very well that 'the day of the Lord will come like a thief in the night'. A thief does not send a warning letter to the house he is about to enter; rather, he surprises the occupants. There will be no warning about the day Christ returns to punish the wicked. That day will be sudden and unexpected.

'As it was in the days of Noah, so it will be at the coming of the Son of Man. For in the days before the flood, people were eating and drinking, marrying and giving in marriage, up to the day Noah entered the ark; and they knew nothing about what would happen until the flood came and took them all away. That is how it will be at the coming of the Son of Man. Two men will be in the field; one will be taken and the other left. Two women will be grinding with a hand mill; one will be taken and the other left.

'Therefore keep watch, because you do not know on what day your Lord will come. But understand this: If the owner of the house had known at what time of night the thief was coming, he would have kept watch and would not have let his house be broken into. So you also must be ready, because the Son of Man will come at an hour when you do not expect him' (Matt. 24:37-44).

The day of the Lord will take unbelievers by complete surprise. While they are speaking to one another about 'peace and safety', destruction will 'come on them suddenly'. As they go about their daily lives, sunk in a deadly spiritual apathy, the wrath of God will unexpectedly sweep them away.

Unbelievers only believe what they can see. As they cannot

see the judgement of God approaching, they dismiss it as fantasy or scaremongering. They encourage each other with false hopes when they talk optimistically about the future, unaware that eternal damnation is on the horizon and about to engulf them. They are not realistic about what is going to happen. They are deaf to the warnings of God, absorbed in their own selfishness, and utterly blind to the judgement that is hanging over them. In every sense they are unprepared for that fast-approaching day.

The 'destruction' that Paul mentions is the 'everlasting destruction' of 2 Thessalonians 1:9-10, when those who do not know God or obey the gospel will be punished 'with everlasting destruction and shut out from the presence of the Lord and from the majesty of his power, on the day he comes to be glorified in his holy people and to be marvelled at among all those who have believed'. It is the utter hopelessness of a Godless existence and an eternal ruin.

> For Christians, these few verses should put urgency in our hearts to win people for Christ. There is only heaven and hell on that day and nothing else.

This destruction is as inevitable 'as labour pains on a pregnant woman', and there will be no escape. When Christ returns it will be too late to repent and believe. All who have rejected Christ will be summoned to the bar of God to receive their condemnation.

For Christians, these few verses should put urgency in our hearts to win people for Christ. There is only heaven and hell on that day and nothing else. May God stir us into action to pray and preach and witness, knowing that the eternal destiny of our neighbours, friends and family is at stake.

Sons of the day or sons of the night? (vv. 4-8)

In these verses Paul contrasts believers, who are the sons of light, with those who belong to the darkness.

Fear not

Contrary to unbelievers, the Thessalonians need not fear that this day will surprise them like a thief, because they are not in 'darkness'. This darkness is a reference to those who are spiritually blind and ignorant, the wicked and careless, who have no thought for their souls. All who are trapped in the darkness of sin and unbelief will be caught out by that day, for they cannot see it approaching, nor do they care about its coming.

The Thessalonians, however, will not be terrorized by the day of the Lord, nor will they be surprised by it. It will not steal in on them and destroy their reward, but be a day of light and joy. Why? Because they are 'sons of the light and sons of the day'. They live in the light, and so will see the day coming and welcome it as the final triumph. The 'light' and 'day' point to the knowledge of Christ in salvation that they have already experienced. The light of redemption shines in their hearts and therefore they are destined for everlasting light.

As Christians we are a 'chosen people, a royal priesthood, a holy nation, a people belonging to God', that we 'may declare the praises of him who called us out of darkness into his wonderful light' (1 Peter 2:9). We must not hold a vain curiosity concerning the day and hour of Christ's return, but wait for it with a holy anticipation and prepare ourselves for its arrival. We must live in the light and behave as children of the light, for 'we do not belong to the night or to the darkness'.

'The night is nearly over; the day is almost here. So let us put aside the deeds of darkness and put on the armour of light' (Rom. 13:12). What does Paul mean? The apostle explains it in the next verses: 'Let us behave decently, as in the daytime, not in orgies and drunkenness, not in sexual immorality and debauchery, not in dissension and jealousy. Rather, clothe yourself with the Lord Jesus Christ, and do not think about how to gratify the desires of the sinful nature' (Rom. 13:13-14).

Be alert and self-controlled

It is unnatural to sleep when the midday sun is shining in our eyes, so it is unnatural to sleep spiritually now that we are children of the light. Sleep is natural to those who live in darkness, for it is the sleep of being insensible and helplessly unaware of the judgement to come. But Christians must not be like that. Instead, we are to be:

'ALERT.' We are to be watchful, sober and spiritually awake. As we wait for our Saviour from heaven, we must be morally alert and live a holy life in view of the day of the Lord. We must live on earth in a way that pleases the Lord as we wait for him to take us to heaven. 'Night' is the element and sphere of unbelievers, the time when they sleep and get drunk, which is the opposite of being spiritually and morally awake. In many ways, the uncertainty about the date of Christ's second coming should make Christians more watchful.

'SELF-CONTROLLED.' We must be filled with a moral and spiritual earnestness, calm and steady in our faith and actions, and faithfully performing our duty as we look forward to that day.

Jesus gave his disciples this warning: 'Be careful, or your hearts will be weighed down with dissipation, drunkenness and the anxieties of life, and that day will close on you unexpectedly like a trap. For it will come upon all those who live on the face of the whole earth. Be always on the watch, and pray that you may be able to escape all that is about to happen, and that you may be able to stand before the Son of Man' (Luke 21:34-36).

Put on faith, love and hope

As the Thessalonians 'belong to the day', they must behave accordingly. They are told for a second time to be 'self-controlled'. In other words, they must watch over their hearts and lives in the same way as an armed soldier standing on guard is careful not to get drunk or fall asleep, which would not only be a dereliction of duty, but dangerous to himself and the people he is meant to be protecting.

Paul exhorts them to put on the whole spiritual armour of God. Faith and love act as a breastplate that protects the heart, and the hope of salvation is a helmet that guards the mind. Faith is that certain knowledge of God, his promises and salvation; love is a yielding to God in joyful obedience; and hope, which looks to the future, is an assurance of salvation which goes hand in hand with obedience. The breastplate and helmet are the spiritual defence we have against the world. With them in place, we shall be ready for the day of Christ's return.

Appointed to receive salvation (vv. 9-10)

Our calling proves that God has not destined us to suffer his just and eternal wrath against sin. Instead, as children of the light, he has appointed us 'to receive salvation through our Lord Jesus Christ'. God has chosen us to enjoy his grace and mercy for ever. He is the source of our salvation and Jesus Christ is its only mediator.

When Paul uses the word 'receive' he reminds us how important it was for us to accept the gift of salvation from God.

The purpose of Christ's atoning death was that, whether we are alive or dead at the parousia, 'we may live together with him'. To live in his perfect presence and to commune eternally with him is our highest joy.

Encourage one another (v. 11)

Paul urges the Thessalonians to believe all that he has said about the second coming of Christ and to 'encourage one another' with its truth. They must allay each other's fears about missing out on eternal life, comfort the downcast who have lost loved ones, and exhort the careless to behave in a manner worthy of their calling.

When we talk to one another about God's word we are strengthened spiritually, which in turn increases our assurance of salvation.

FOR FURTHER STUDY

1. Read the parable of the ten virgins in Matthew 25:1-13. Try to understand the meaning of the parable. What are the main differences between the wise and foolish virgins? How should we live to be like the wise virgins?

2. What is the main point that Jesus is making in the parable of the talents in Matthew 25:14-30?

3. In Mark 13:32-37 Jesus exhorts his disciples to 'keep watch'. What are some of the ways we can 'keep watch' in preparation for the second coming?

TO THINK ABOUT AND DISCUSS

1. Read Ephesians 5:8-20 and discuss how we are to live as children of the light. Describe the main characteristics of a person who 'belongs to the night or to the darkness'.

2. Explain the differences between faith, love and hope.

3. How can we encourage others more effectively? How can we encourage them to be 'alert and self-controlled'?

4. Give each member of your group an opportunity to explain why the second coming of Christ is so important.

14 Love one another

(5:12-15)

It is so important that we put the word of God into practice. It is the easiest thing in the world to read the Scriptures and then to ignore what they say.

We should be like the faithful dog whose eyes and ears were all the time watching and listening for words of command from his master, who was walking with a friend along the top of a cliff. While deep in conversation, the master began gesticulating. He raised his arm in the direction of a precipice. The faithful dog, thinking his master was giving a word of command to him, instantly leapt to his death over the precipice. If only we were as quick to obey our Master's commands!

A missionary translator was struggling to find a word for 'obedience' in the native language. As he returned home from the village one day, he whistled for his dog and it came running to him at full speed. An old native, who was watching, said admiringly in the native tongue, 'Your dog is all ear.' Immediately the missionary knew that the word obedience should be translated 'all ear'.

In response to Timothy's encouraging report, Paul wants the Thessalonians to be 'all ear'. He wants the watchfulness and soberness of the preceding verses to become part of their everyday lives and for them to practise what he has been preaching. With this in mind he passes on some strikingly brief directions, saying much in just a few words.

Love your leaders (vv. 12-13)

Paul is probably referring to the church elders whom he appointed when he was in Thessalonica. It appears that some of the members were not keen to obey the rules of the leaders, and Paul is urging them to 'respect' these men for the following reasons:

THEY 'WORK HARD AMONG YOU'. They are men who exert themselves for your benefit and edification amid great difficulty. They instruct, comfort and guide you in the things of God, sometimes to the point of weariness.

THEY 'ARE OVER YOU IN THE LORD'. God has appointed them to be your leaders, which is reason enough to respect them.

THEY 'ADMONISH YOU'. They urge you, both privately and publicly, to obey God by giving you much-needed encouragement, but also reproof and remonstrance when necessary.

The Thessalonians are to value their office and highly esteem their person 'because of their work'. The leaders of a church edify believers, build up the kingdom of God, save souls by God's power, and prepare its members for the return of Christ. There is no greater work; therefore, they must be highly thought of, loved and honoured by all who sit under their ministry.

One of the best ways we can love our leaders is to 'live in peace' with them. Paul tells the Thessalonians to be affectionately loyal to their leaders. Instead of arguing with and criticizing those who admonish them, they must treat them with the respect they deserve.

Love one another (vv. 14-15)

We not only have a responsibility to love our leaders, but to love one another as well. Every individual in the church should be loved and respected, and when necessary warned. The following general instructions are for all the members of the church, not just the leaders:

'WARN THOSE WHO ARE IDLE.' Charles Spurgeon says that 'the most likely man to go to hell is the man who has nothing to do on earth. Idle people tempt the devil to tempt them. If I throw myself down in idleness, like an old piece of iron, I must not wonder that I grow rusty with sin.' The idle are those who are out of step with others, like soldiers who do not keep ranks. They are loafers and meddlers, who refuse to work and expect others to look after them. They must be warned to live God-honouring lives and to earn the bread they eat. They certainly must not be supported in their laziness.

'ENCOURAGE THE TIMID.' The fainthearted, who are worried about their dead relatives and friends and about their own salvation, must not be despised, but comforted and encouraged.

'HELP THE WEAK.' The spiritually immature who are tempted to lapse into immorality must not be abandoned, but given all the necessary spiritual and moral assistance to help them stand strong for Christ.

'BE PATIENT WITH EVERYONE.' The word patience means to hold out for a long time before taking action. Paul wants the Thessalonians to be longsuffering towards those in the church and those who are outsiders, even if they are mistreating them. They must not reject anyone. Bear and forbear is his command.

These instructions are another way of saying that we should look not only to our own interests, but also to the interest of others (Phil. 2:4).

Paul then condemns paying back evil for evil, which is the complete opposite of what Jesus taught and did. Retaliation is never justified—we must forgive as we have been forgiven. As in all things we have the perfect example of Jesus Christ, who 'committed no sin, and no deceit was found in his mouth. When they hurled their insults at him, he did not retaliate; when he suffered, he made no threats. Instead, he entrusted himself to him who judges justly' (1 Peter 2:22-23).

> Retaliation is never justified—we must forgive as we have been forgiven. As in all things we have the perfect example of Jesus Christ who 'committed no sin, and no deceit was found in his mouth. When they hurled their insults at him, he did not retaliate; when he suffered, he made no threats. Instead, he entrusted himself to him who judges justly' (1 Peter 2:22-23).

If we take revenge, we are as foolish as the man who drove his brand new car into an old parked car. When the police asked him to explain his actions, he replied by saying that both cars belonged to him and he was taking revenge on his old car for giving him so much trouble.

What should our reaction be if we are mistreated? We should certainly not imitate the pious but cranky old woman whose neighbours forgot to ask her to their picnic. On the morning of the event they suddenly realized their affront and sent a small boy round to her house with a special invitation. 'It's too late now,' she snapped, 'I've already prayed for rain!' On the contrary, we should 'always try to be kind'. Simply to avoid retribution is not enough. All resentment should be extinguished by a loving kindness that seeks to repay evil with good.

FOR FURTHER STUDY

1. Read Hebrews 13:17. How should we behave in order to make our leaders' work 'a joy'?
2. Paul gave the Thessalonians a similar admonition about idleness in his second letter. Read 2 Thessalonians 3:6-15. How should we treat a Christian brother or sister who is idle?
3. Read Matthew 5:43-48, Romans 12:9-21 and 1 Peter 3:8-12. List some of the practical ways we can love others.

TO THINK ABOUT AND DISCUSS

1. Think of some Scriptures that might encourage the timid.
2. What does the Bible say about helping the weak?
3. To retaliate is a natural reaction of people in our modern society. How can Christians guard against reacting in a vindictive and retaliatory way? How did Paul respond when he was persecuted?
4. Why is it important to be 'patient with everyone'?

15 The will of God

(5:16-22)

Christians are often perplexed about the will of God, but in these verses Paul gives the Thessalonians some very important duties that are clearly God's will.

God's will (vv. 16-18)

Here is God's will in three specific areas which affect our everyday lives. These instructions must direct our hearts and lives to live more fully for his glory.

'BE JOYFUL ALWAYS.' The great composer, Joseph Haydn, was once asked why his church music was so cheerful. He replied, 'When I think upon God, my heart is so full of joy that the notes dance and leap, as it were, from my pen, and since God has given me a cheerful heart it will be pardoned me that I serve him with a cheerful spirit.' A Christian's joy is not a natural joy that ebbs and flows according to the circumstances that surround us, but a supernatural joy that comes from God and is rooted in our relationship with him.

It is a joy that fills our hearts even in the midst of persecution. Joy was one of the marks of primitive Christianity, which amazed the heathen world and attracted men to Christ. Paul is concerned that the joy of the Thessalonians might be strangled by suffering, so he urges them to rejoice not in what was happening to them, but in their Saviour and all that he has done for them.

'PRAY CONTINUALLY.' Martin Luther, when pressed by huge volumes of work, did not use it as an excuse to stop praying, but said, 'I have so much to do that I cannot get on without three hours a day of praying.' The way to rejoice always is to pray continually and to have a close walk with the giver of joy. We must cultivate a spirit of constant devotion so that our lives are filled with the presence of God. Prayer is a lifting up of our hearts to God in humble submission and dependence, trusting him as our loving Father and acknowledging him as our almighty Lord. Paul is encouraging the Thessalonians to take hold of God in every situation and at all times, to draw near to him especially in times of conflict, and to develop an intimate relationship with him.

> Martin Luther, when pressed by huge volumes of work, did not use it as an excuse to stop praying, but said, 'I have so much to do that I cannot get on without three hours a day of praying.'

'GIVE THANKS IN ALL CIRCUMSTANCES.' George Matheson, the Scottish minister and hymnwriter, who was practically blind at eighteen, once prayed, 'My God, I have never thanked you for my "thorn". I have thanked you a thousand times for my roses, but never once for my "thorn". I have been looking forward to a world where I shall get compensation for my cross as itself a present glory. Teach me the glory of my cross; teach me the value of my "thorn". Show me that I have climbed to you by the path of pain. Show me that my tears have made my rainbow.' Thanksgiving to God is to be given in adversity and prosperity, for no matter what happens all things work together for the believer's good. To be thankful is a fruit of grace and is in contrast to the constant grumblings and ingratitude of a godless world. For Christians there is no situation in which we cannot give thanks. Even in affliction we are more than conquerors as the Spirit of glory and of God rests on us. In our blessings we would do well to remember the Chinese proverb, 'When you drink from the stream, remember the spring.' A life of prayer and devotion leads to a thankful heart.

The Spirit's fire (vv. 19-22)

Paul does not want the Thessalonians to smother or suppress the supernatural workings of God's Spirit in their midst by being insensitive to what God is doing. He is specifically referring to the gift of prophecy, the forth-telling or fore-telling of God's word, which is a burning flame in the church and must not be extinguished. When the gift is used properly it strengthens, encourages and comforts the church. Prophecies must not be treated with contempt otherwise the Holy Spirit, who imparts the gift, is dishonoured and belittled.

However, the Thessalonians must not go to the opposite

extreme and accept everything that is said in a prophetic way. They must 'test everything' to see if it is in accordance with God's written revelation in the Old Testament. If it does not agree with God's word, they must throw it out. If it does agree with the Scriptures, they must 'hold on' to it and be thankful for it. Perhaps the gift was being misused to predict the date of the second coming of Christ, and Paul is exhorting them to use their spiritual discernment so they do not throw out the good with the bad.

'Avoid every kind of evil' is an exhortation to reject all sorts of evil, whether it comes through a spurious revelation, which is designed to ensnare them, or through the wicked example of someone's life that tempts them to do wrong. Whatever the evil, it must be vigorously avoided, which in turn will protect them from being led astray.

These last instructions are connected to the previous paragraph. It is the Holy Spirit who enables us to pray, rejoice and give thanks, and who gives us a thirst for the things of God.

For further study ▶

FOR FURTHER STUDY

1. Paul practised what he preached. When he was in prison he set the believers an example to follow by his exhortations and way of life. Read Philippians 1:3-26 and highlight Paul's example to the Philippians in the areas of prayer, joy and thanksgiving.
2. There are many different beliefs about spiritual gifts in the church today. Read 1 Corinthians 14:1-12 and, without prejudice, consider what Paul is saying to the church in the twenty-first century.

TO THINK ABOUT AND DISCUSS

1. Why should a Christian be joyful always? Give as many reasons as you can.
2. Discuss the best ways to develop your own prayer life and the prayer life of your group. What are some of the things that stifle prayer? Why is prayer so important?
3. There are many Christians who are always complaining about something. How can we encourage them to be more thankful?
4. Name some examples of the Spirit's power in the Book of Acts.

16 God is faithful

(5:23-28)

Paul concludes his letter by showing the Thessalonians just how desperately they need God, who is the source of power for the believer. Without God equipping and transforming us to live the lives he has called us to live, we can do nothing for his glory and we shall not be able to stand before him on the Day of Judgement.

God's sanctification (vv. 23-24)

Paul refers to God as the 'God of peace' not only because he is the author of peace, but because his redeeming grace in the death of Christ brings spiritual peace to the heart and mind of the believer. Paul asks the God of peace to sanctify the Thessalonians 'through and through'. He does not want any part of their being to fall short of entire consecration to God. He wants them to be separate from a life of sin and fully dedicated to the glory of God. This is the radical and perfect holiness that only God provides, a holiness that is not yet fully realized, but shall be ours when Christ returns. The Puritan Joseph Caryl put it this way, 'Perfect holiness is the aim of the saints on earth, and it is the reward of the saints in heaven.'

> When every part of our lives, inward and outward, lies under the sanctifying grace and power of God, we shall be 'kept blameless at the coming of our Lord Jesus Christ'. Those who are sanctified will be kept free from sin and impurity and declared to be without flaw at Christ's return.

When every part of our lives, inward and outward, lies under the sanctifying grace and power of God, we shall be 'kept blameless at the coming of our Lord Jesus Christ'. Those who are sanctified will be kept free from sin and impurity and declared to be without flaw at Christ's return. They will be preserved from the condemnation that overtakes the wicked on the Day of Judgement and, in its place, will enjoy the glory to be revealed at that time.

Paul is not teaching sinless perfection, but urging the Thessalonians to give themselves entirely to God so they can be changed into his likeness and made ready for the parousia. It is a similar sentiment to Jude's: 'To him who is able to keep you from falling and to present you before his glorious presence without fault and with great joy' (Jude 24).

The prayer that Paul offers is based on God's character. God is trustworthy in every respect and so all believers are secure in him. We have invincible confidence, as our hope does not rest on our own efforts to live up to God's standards, but on the faithfulness of God, who never fails to fulfil his promises or to keep his covenant. In other words, it is not our feeble hold of God that makes us secure, but God's strong hold of us. That is why our hope is not in vain. That is why we need not fear the approaching Day of Judgement. Our certainty is wrapped up in God, who will complete what he has begun. Our sanctification and preservation are guaranteed in him.

Such a confidence, however, must never lead to moral laxity, for a true reception of God's grace leads to a heartfelt determination to obey his commands. A carpenter, when a workmate questioned the correctness of some work he was doing on a building, pulled out a notebook and looked at it. 'I am obeying instructions,' he said. 'I'm not the contractor, but I'm going by the book.' A little later, when he was ridiculing his friend for not working on the Sabbath, he was surprised to receive his own reply, 'I am going by the Book. Someone else is responsible for the final outcome; all I have to do is obey instructions.' If the safest way to build a house is to obey instructions, how much more should we obey God's instructions when building our lives?

Paul's exhortations (vv. 25-28)

Paul and his fellow missionaries are not so proud or foolish as to think they can serve God without help from their friends, so they exhort the Thessalonians to pray for them. In short, they urgently entreat their brothers and sisters in Christ to uphold them before the throne of grace. Paul knows from personal experience the power of prayer, especially in all the difficulties he has encountered. Thomas Watson underlined the effectiveness of prayer when he said, 'The angel fetched Peter out of prison, but it was prayer that fetched the angel.'

As Paul is absent from the Thessalonians he wants to pass on his final greetings to everyone, making sure no one is overlooked. When he says they should greet all the brothers 'with a holy kiss', which was the normal mode of greeting, he is in effect saying, 'Pass on my love to all the brothers.' This 'holy kiss' is equivalent to our warm handshake and is a sign and seal of Christian love.

He then gives the Thessalonians a solemn charge, which implies a divine punishment if it is not carried out. His letter, which contains important teaching, encouragement and admonition, must be read to everyone in the congregation, even to those who do not want to hear it because they fear it might contain an injunction against them. Perhaps Paul wanted it to be read out during a time of public worship.

Paul's farewell benediction ends the letter as he began it, with one of his favourite themes: 'grace', God's unmerited favour to us in Christ.

FOR FURTHER STUDY

1. The faithfulness of God is a theme that runs throughout the Bible. Read Deuteronomy 32:3-4; Psalm 33:4-5; 145:8-16; 1 Corinthians 10:13. What exactly is the faithfulness of God? How has it been demonstrated in your life?

2. Paul mentions prayer on so many occasions in his letters. When others pray for us, why is it such an encouragement?

3. Paul often ends his letters by mentioning grace. See 1 Corinthians 16:23; 2 Corinthians 13:14; Galatians 6:18; Ephesians 6:24; Philippians 4:23; Colossians 4:18 and so on. Why is grace so important to him?

TO THINK ABOUT AND DISCUSS

1. What is the main theme of Paul's first letter to the Thessalonians?

2. What have you learnt from 1 Thessalonians? What has challenged you? What has encouraged you? What has rebuked you?

3. Discuss any practical steps you can take to put into practice what you have learnt.

Additional resources

G. K. Beale, *The IVP New Testament Commentary Series: 1 & 2 Thessalonians*, IVP

John Calvin, *Calvin's Commentaries: Commentary of the First Epistle to the Thessalonians*, Baker Book House

Gene L. Green, *The Pillar New Testament Commentary: The Letters to the Thessalonians*, Eerdmans, Apollos

William Hendriksen, *New Testament Commentary: 1 & 2 Thessalonians*, Banner of Truth

John MacArthur, *The MacArthur New Testament Commentary: 1 & 2 Thessalonians*, Moody Publications

Richard Mayhue, *Focus on the Bible: 1 & 2 Thessalonians*, Christian Focus

Leon Morris, *Tyndale New Testament Commentaries: 1 & 2 Thessalonians*, IVP

Charles C. Ryrie, *Everyman's Bible Commentary: 1 & 2 Thessalonians*, Moody Publications

Charles A. Wanamaker, *NIGTC: The Epistles to the Thessalonians*, Eerdmans

Andrew W. Young, *Let's Study 1 & 2 Thessalonians*, Banner of Truth

OPENING UP 1 THESSALONIANS

OPENING UP 1 THESSALONIANS

The Opening up series

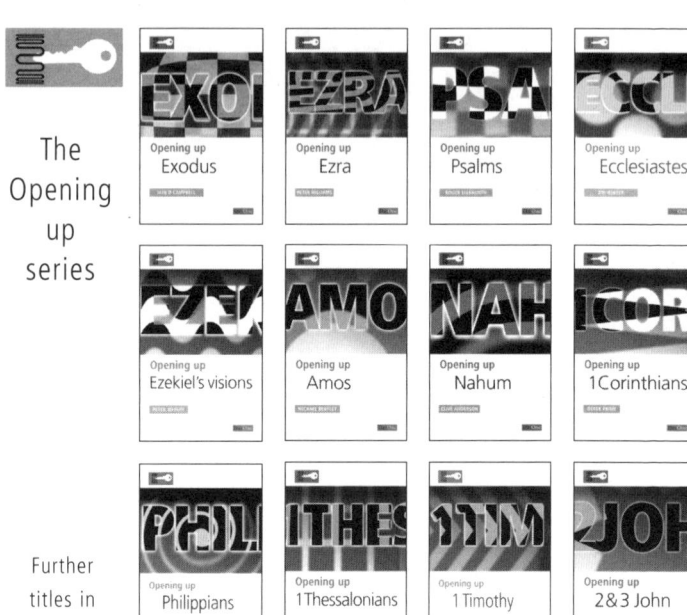

Further titles in preparation

This fine series is aimed at the 'average person in the church' and combines brevity, accuracy and readability with an attractive page layout. Thought-provoking questions make the books ideal for both personal or small group use.

'Laden with insightful quotes and penetrating practical application, Opening up Philippians is a Bible study tool which belongs on every Christian's bookshelf!'

DR. PHIL ROBERTS, PRESIDENT, MIDWESTERN BAPTIST THEOLOGICAL SEMINARY, KANSAS CITY, M I S S O U R I

Please contact us for a free catalogue

In the UK ☎ 01568 613 740   **email**— sales@dayone.co.uk

In the United States: ☎ Toll Free:1-8-morebooks

In Canada: ☎ 519 763 0339 www.dayone.co.uk